Knit, Purl, and Design!

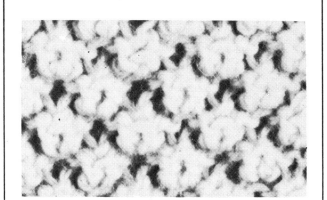

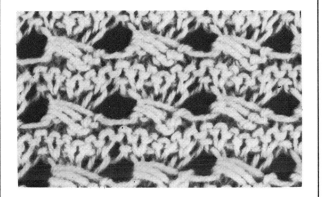

Knit, Purl, and Design!

Annette Feldman

Harper & Row, Publishers

New York, Evanston, San Francisco,
London

All stitch directions in this book have been thoroughly checked for accuracy. We cannot, however, be responsible for misinterpretation of directions or variations caused by the individual's working techniques.

FIRST EDITION
STANDARD BOOK NUMBER: 06-011219-0
LIBRARY OF CONGRESS CATALOG CARD NUMBER: 72-79662

Contents

Guide rules are offered from a designer's notebook, imparting to you complete knowledge on proportion, balance, shaping, and all other details involved in the creating of your own designs. A standard-body size measurement chart is given here, with suggested basic measurements for twenty-six different sizes, ranging from the six-month-infant size to size 46 for men.

Translations are given of many knitting terms for those who choose to use our patterns but are more familiar with the terminology in their native language, and for those who would like to adapt their own knitting to designs and directions appearing in foreign periodicals.

1

The history and legend of knitting

Over two thousand years ago, someone discovered that the use of a strand of fiber and something to work it around made it possible to produce a strong, even length of woven material, and that the strand of fiber and probably the use of someone's four fingers on the left hand as a tool was the very start of the hand-knitting craft.

We know that the craft is indeed not a recently discovered one. Actually its earliest known practice dates back to the fourth century B.C. Discovered only lately in an Egyptian tomb dating to that time is, among other possessions, a pair of thick hand-knit woolen socks. Other discoveries, however, indicate that perhaps even those woolen socks were not among the earliest things to have been hand-knitted. Findings in Arabia dating back to the second century indicate that there was in that part of the world a well-advanced knowledge of both technique and designing principles. This would lead us to believe that the craft had started there long before, and that somewhere there is more evidence yet undiscovered and dating back even further than the fourth century B.C. A pair of very old well-made red sandal socks made in Arabia and now in the Victoria and Albert Museum in London shows proof of such advanced knowledge as the "turning of a heel" and "dividing stitches for the big toe."

Some very fine maroon and gold silk knitting also made in Arabia in very early days depicts a beauty and technique almost unsurpassed, even by some of the wonderful work being done today.

With communication and travel being slow and difficult in those early days, it was not until many centuries later that a knowledge of the hand-knitting skill was transmitted to other parts of the world. Some work began to appear in England and Scotland during the late fourteenth century, probably brought over from the Middle East by sailors and soldiers returning home. Strong interest was shown there at once in this new way of making goods and clothing, and it was in that part of the world that the word "knitting" actually began to evolve. It comes from the Old English "cnyttan," meaning to knot.

Tools were crude and clumsy at first, and from the probable start of "four fingers on the left hand" as the basic tool, early knitters, in search of a better way, came upon the idea of using first a series of pegs arranged in either a single or double row, or in a circle, and then a pair of rods, known as knitting pins, or needles. Of the two newly evolved methods, the latter quickly became by far the more popular, and the peg method was largely discarded. Knitting needles then became the medium for producing this interesting new type of woven fabric, needles hand-hewn from briarwood, copper, ivory and bone, and for very fine work, extremely delicate needles were fashioned of wire.

Knitting in the New World soon became no longer just an interesting craft to experiment with, but rather a skill to be practiced and improved upon as time and experience dictated. It offered a fine way of producing good, functional articles of clothing or yards of goods, comparatively simple and easy to manipulate in the era before the Industrial Revolution, when almost everything was made by hand.

The days of the early Renaissance in Middle Europe were progressive, growing times in many arts, among those, the one of hand-knitting. People liked the skill, found it very worthwhile, and wanted to foster it further. As a result, this type of work rose to its greatest height during those days. Throughout continental Europe, knitting guilds were formed and began to flourish under royal and ecclesiastical patronage. Guild regulations were rigid, and only men could belong. A master hand-knitter needed to pass through many rigorous tests in order to achieve his position in life. He needed to serve first as an apprentice for six years—three years studying under a master and three years as a journeyman knitter. After that he took an examination. In thirteen weeks he had to make and completely finish the following articles: a large and richly textured carpet, a beret, wide and flourishing as was the type worn in those days, a woolen shirt, and a pair of hose with Spanish clocks. If he passed this test, his occupation and income were established for life.

Up to this time women had not yet tried their hand at knitting. This was a man's business and a serious and important one, and the only women who did knit were the widows of master knitters, who were allowed to carry on their husband's work. Slowly and subtly, however, fascinated with what was being done with the clicking of the needles and a ball of yarn, they began to learn how the various techniques were performed. Nuns and laywomen, many of them close family to a master knitter, were the first women to start to knit and to make items of their own, mostly utilitarian, yet many of them things of great beauty, the ladies improvising and improving as they went along.

Eventually, as in much of life, the wheels of progress turned and many changes occurred. As early as 1589, a Reverend William Lee of Calverton, England, had invented a stocking-frame knitting machine so good that many of its basic mechanical principles are still being used in knitting machines today. When he presented it to the English government, however, they refused to give him a patent on his invention because they were afraid it might interfere with the work of the hand-knitters. It was not until much later, in 1750, that machine-knitting finally got started, and soon after that, men began to busy themselves with the new mechanical knitting of socks, gloves, scarfs, tunic cloaks, and everything else that people were wearing at the time. Machine-knitting was prevailing, and from then on most knitting done by men was done on the machine, and it was the women who carried on with the hand-knitting work they had learned. They invented new stitches and continued to make hats and scarfs and sweaters and other things for simple utilitarian warmth for themselves and their families, and occasionally they indulged in a pretty lacy shawl, or perhaps a doily or bedspread with which to beautify their homes.

Knitting techniques and stitches have changed very little over the centuries. Many new stitches have been added, but these always involve only a different manipulation of the same basic stitches. What has changed, however, and only quite recently, is what people are knitting these days. As we know, garments originally consisted mostly of rather plain, utilitarian articles made for warmth and service, with the possible exception of lacy collars and shawls, doilies and afghans, which showed a little more artistic and frivolous bent. The complete emergence of knitting as a genuine high-fashion medium occurred only after World War I. It has now reached the point where much of the most fashionable clothing being worn today is hand-knit, and is so beautiful that few (both men and women) can resist the temptation to make something of their own.

2

Why you should knit

A hobby as simple as the little "knit and purl," which offers so many pleasures and fills so many needs, is one that perhaps none of us should overlook. Knitting is fun, a simple creative skill, absorbing and relaxing at the same time. It is exciting to watch tiny individual stitches multiply and grow into a beautiful whole, and particularly rewarding for you to know that it is you yourself with your own two hands, a pair of needles, and a length of yarn who are causing this beautiful thing to be. So stimulating, actually, is this experience that one who knits is seldom without "work on hand," and just as there is an eagerness to complete one project, so there is usually a strong motivation to go on immediately to the next, and then the next.

The "For Older Women Only" tag has long since been removed from this type of pleasure, as has the oft-common picture of grandmother in her rocker, spectacles on her nose, a pussy cat on her lap, and a pair of knitting needles and a ball of yarn alongside her. Today almost everyone knits—men and women, young and old alike—and those few of us who don't, should. Knitting has always been a popular hobby, but never has its popularity grown to such heights as now in the last half of the twentieth century. The new designs are high-fashion and fun to make, but more importantly,

there seems to be in everyone a search for more ways to relax and to do things for oneself. Days now are high-tensioned, and the pace of life is fast. Some of us can barely keep up with it, and others would like to escape. Our world is flying to the moon and soaring into space, and it has been pressured, indeed, into a very high rate of speed. This is progress as it comes, and progress perhaps as we want it—but progress, too, in such a manner that we are deviously finding ways to counteract it.

It is no secret that one recent counter-reaction to the rate of speed of our progress has been a return to more simple and natural things, which offer in themselves a bit of a chance to slow down and stop to think for a while. Many of us are growing gardens, others are taking pleasure in riding a bike instead of a sports car, in preparing a fabulous casserole at home instead of going out to dinner, and in making a bench from hand-hewn lumber. We are cooking and sewing and baking and mowing, all in the course of our quiet plot to maintain something of our own personalities in a world that we often feel is becoming too strongly automated.

And so we knit and purl, too, for all the reasons we are doing other things. The stitch-by-stitch process and the steady clicking rhythm of the needles offer a feeling of ease and relaxation, almost like that which a baby feels when his carriage is being rocked, or a sailor when riding the gentle waves of the sea. You can take pleasure in this feeling, either when you are alone or in a room with many others. Since knitting is a many-faceted art, there are simple parts with which you can very easily relax, and then there are the more complicated procedures which are totally absorbing and distract the mind from any problems that might exist there. The choice of which type of knitting you enjoy most is entirely up to you. Often you can mix the two, and since a knitted piece is usually a composition of many parts, you can work the simpler parts when you desire the easy, lulling type of relaxation, and the more complex parts when you want to be completely absorbed in your work.

Knitting is also a "portable" hobby, and unlike many others, you can work at it wherever you choose—indoors in front of the television, outdoors on the lawn, at the park while you are watching the children play, or in the car while you are riding—and all the while that you are enjoying yourself and relaxing with this hobby, you are watching six stitches to an inch grow gradually into eight rows to an inch, and then only so many more inches to complete your project. Much as the single notes on a piano join one to another to create a lovely melody, so your stitches grow sooner than you know into a beautiful finished whole—a thing often of great beauty, sometimes even an heirloom piece to be passed down from one generation to the next.

Those of you who have knitted before have certainly already experienced the pleasures of this fascinating craft, and those of you who have never knitted should indulge yourselves as soon as you possibly can, and come to experience many happy hours of simple pleasure and contentment. The following chapter enumerates and describes the wealth of beautiful things that can be made, and our Knitter's Guide in Chapter 7 will tell you just how to get started.

3

What you should knit

Knitting is so versatile an art, and the choice of things to make so myriad, that it is perhaps best to provide a categorical list of the wide variety of things you might want to make for yourself, your family, and as gifts for your friends. The list of clothing, as you will see, runs a complete gamut, ranging from cuddly infant swaddling outfits to big exciting he-man ski sweaters, and encompassing everything else in between. There are also suggestions for lovely things to make for the home and for interesting small gift items. So comprehensive is the list, that it resembles, to some degree, the directory in a major department store.

Perusing a list may not be too inspiring, but look for a moment at our photographs of beautiful pattern stitches and try to imagine any of the things you might choose to make in one of those pattern stitches, envisioning also the wealth of exciting colors and materials available for you to work with. Also, as you contemplate the list of items, be assured that, as you read on through the book, you will have no need to be concerned with the apparent ease or complexity of whatever it is you have chosen to make. We have tried in both our Knitter's Guide and Designer's Guide (Chapters 7 and 8) to explain as simply as possible all the techniques involved in whatever it is you are going to

knit, and to make the doing of it a pleasurable experience for you. Beyond this, there is only one bit of advice we want to give. If you are a brand-new knitter, or a normally impatient person, you might be wise to begin with something of smaller, rather than larger dimension, so that your project will take less time to complete, and you will be able more quickly to see and enjoy the fruit of your labor—and then be encouraged to go on to something else.

THINGS TO KNIT FOR INFANTS AND BABIES

Afghans	Diaper sets
Bibs	Dresses
Blankets	Mittens
Booties	Pram robes
Bottle warmers	Sacques
Buntings	Snow suits
Capes	Soakers
Carriage robes	Sweaters

THINGS TO KNIT FOR SMALL CHILDREN

Bathing suits	Scarfs
Bathrobes	Skating outfits
Capes	Skirts
Coats	Snow suits
Dresses	Socks
Gloves	Suits
Hats	Sweaters
Mittens	Vests

THINGS TO KNIT FOR WOMEN AND GIRLS

Bags	Jackets
Bathing suits	Mittens
Belts	Scarfs
Blouses	Skirts
Capes	Slacks
Coats	Suits
Dresses	Sweaters
Hats	Vests

THINGS TO KNIT FOR MEN AND BOYS

Caps	Shirts
Gloves	Slippers
Mittens	Socks
Jackets	Sweaters
Ponchos	Ties
Scarfs	Vests

THINGS TO KNIT FOR YOUR HOME

Afghans	Pillows
Bathroom accessories	Place mats
Bedspreads	Potholders
Closet accessories	Rugs
Doilies	Slip seat covers
Kitchen accessories	Wall hangings

THINGS TO KNIT FOR SMALL GIFTS

Book covers	Golf club covers
Bookmarks	Kerchiefs
Bottle covers	Key rings
Coasters	Pillow covers
Dog blankets	Purse accessories
Doilies	Tennis racquet covers

4

You can design your own knits

How do you start? For those of you who have never knitted before, our Knitter's Guide in Chapter 7 will explain to you just how to begin. Your basic tools, for a start, will be a pair of knitting needles and a ball of yarn, any color, any size. We show and tell you how to hold the needles in your hands, how to set your yarn onto the needles, how to make your first stitches, and then how to go on. We ask you to practice a little with doing just this, and when you are satisfied with what you have done, you will find more information in that same section on how to increase and decrease for shaping, and how to bind off or remove all of your stitches from both needles and finish off when your work is done. When you have accomplished this much, you are already a knitter.

Other information on knitting techniques that you, as well as many much more advanced knitters, might want or need to know also appears in our Knitter's Guide, such as how to manipulate certain stitches, and how to pick up stitches, form button-holes, work hemlines, seam, block, and do practically everything else. Knitters all now, what is it you would like to make?

With the help of our How to Design pages which follow next in Chapter 5 and our Designer's Guide (Chapter 8), you can make pretty much whatever you want. It could be something you've admired in a store window, or a copy of one of your favorite pieces of clothing, or a completely original design of a garment you've always thought about wearing. It is both fun and a challenge to design original things of your own, and with the knitting and designing knowledge you gain as you read on, and the aid of our photographs with complete instructions for over three hundred interesting pattern stitches appearing in Chapter 6, and the beautiful yarns available in the stores, you are ready to start out on one of the most exciting and rewarding projects of your life.

You now might possibly begin to wonder how you will know if your design is a good one. If you have some doubt, be reassured by knowing that the art of design consists really of just what you like and feel is in good taste. Once upon a time there were very strict and rigid rules governing design principles. A sweater or dress needed to be exactly a certain length, plump people never wore bold patterns, and the combination of pink and orange or lavender and brown was considered a disaster, color-wise. Major designers in all areas have changed this, however, perhaps tongue-in-cheek to begin with, or perhaps just as a natural reaction to the stuffiness of the old world. As a result of this changed attitude, a reign of complete freedom in both dress and design has occurred, and the world has perhaps bettered some for it. Wear your clothes at whatever length you choose—your dresses and skirts above the knee, to the knee, below the knee, mid-calf, ankle length, or to the floor; your sweaters finger-tip length, hip length, waist length, or just below the bosom. Whatever pleases you most, and whatever you feel the need for, that is what is best, and that is what you want. If you are plump, accentuate your positive with as bold a pattern as you like, and if you are very lean, don't hesitate to vertical-stripe your creation just because you think it will make you look more lean. Perhaps that is rather the better way for you to look. The pink-and-orange color combination turns out to cast one of the sunniest hues of color, while the lavender and brown projects a very subtle moodiness.

Some of you possibly prefer a tighter rein in designing your first project and would like someone to tell you exactly what to do. This might perhaps be an easier beginning for you, and if your doubts are very strong, compromise and select a garment with instructions from a current knitting periodical —but add to it a little something of your own, such as a change of the color and a more appealing pattern stitch. In this way you will gain more reassurance to go on with your own designing later on. For those, however, who are more adventurous, rest assured that whatever it is you decide to make —your own style, your own stitch, and your own color or combination of colors will be a good design and hopefully even a great one.

In the pages following in our How to Design section, you will find a suggested standard body size measurement chart and a simply detailed explanation of the basic steps in design procedure. Read it carefully, almost as a lesson. When you have done this, decide what it is you want to make, choose a pattern stitch, select yarn, remember what you have read about How to Design, and refer as often as you need to our Knitter's Guide and our Designer's Guide. When you have finished your creation, you will be the first to say, "I designed and made it myself," and to know and enjoy what a wonderful feeling of creation this is.

5

How to design

The art of designing beautiful knitwear stems from, in addition to your own good taste, the interesting and very rudimentary lessons of addition, subtraction, multiplication, and division, sometimes all, and sometimes just one or two of these exercises. Your basic involvements are simply the mathematics of your body measurements, or if you are making a straight piece such as a scarf, a rug, or an afghan, the size of that piece, multiplied by the tension or gauge (number of stitches per inch) you have decided to work with, and the accommodation of your final sum to the multiple of stitches necessary to work out the particular pattern you are using. Though it is not at all a difficult skill to acquire, as elementary almost as the lessons in a grade school arithmetic class, still it is rather exciting to see your simple calculations work to create a new hand-knit design.

Your first step in designing is to decide what it is you want to knit. Let us assume that it is an afghan —a beautiful, very functional and worthwhile project to attempt and, despite its size, one of the most simple things to make. There is no standard size for afghans; they can be as large or as small as you want. More often than not, they are rectangular in shape, and also, more often than not, the length will be a minimum of 12 inches more than the width,

or a maximum of 20 inches more. Popular sizes are 48″ x 60″, 54″ x 66″, 60″ x 74″, and 70″ x 84″— although, be reminded once more, there is no standard size.

You need yarn and a pair of needles, and a decision once more as to just what kind of afghan you want to make. Look carefully through our group of over three hundred pattern stitches and pick the one that you like best, deciding now whether you prefer a richly textured stitch, or a gossamer, lacy pattern, or perhaps a combination of a texture and a cable stitch pattern. Since afghans are basically large pieces, they are usually worked in strips or squares, and then the pieces are joined together, either by sewing or by using a simple crochet stitch; for this reason the use of more than one type of stitch is quite feasible, as is also the use of more than one color. Actually, the combination of several stitches or colors adds much interest to your piece. In making the selection of your stitch, refer to the list of abbreviations and the few important notes immediately preceding all of the stitch photographs, and refer also to the Knitter's Guide for questions you might have concerning how to work any particular stitch.

Presume now that you have decided to make a lacy afghan, 60″ wide x 72″ long, that you would like to make it in three shades of one color, and that you have selected a pattern stitch with a multiple of 4. At this time you should select your yarn, determining whether you want your afghan to be a lighter rather than a heavier weight, whether you want to make it out of wool or one of the many new machine-washable synthetics, and if you prefer a solid yarn, a textured one, or a soft fluffy mohair type. A trip to your local yarn shop will show you what is available, what the prices and advantages of each are, and what the color range is in the yarn you finally decide to use.

You know that you want your afghan in three shades of a color, and you've just about decided that you want it to range from a light shade to a medium one, and then to a fairly deep one, and that you want to use more of the deep shade than the other two. You do not know how much yarn you will be using, but since most yarns have a dye lot number, you must be certain that you have a sufficient amount of the particular dye lot you are using to complete your project. Most yarn shopkeepers will be able to estimate roughly what your requirements will be, and are willing to give you the assurance that if you have bought too much, they will accept for return whatever is left over, and that if you have bought only a starting amount, they will lay away enough of that same dye lot so that you can pick up the remainder as you need it. In either case, your one obligation is to let the shopkeeper know, as soon as possible, how much yarn you are actually going to need, and this you can determine after you have completed approximately one-quarter of your work. Multiplying the amount used by 4, you can have a reasonably fair calculation of the entire amount that you will need. If you add to this amount an extra ball or two for "spare," you are in a position to complete your yarn order with the knowledge that you will finish your work with the same dye lot with which you started.

You now have your design roughly in mind, and your yarn on hand. It is time to determine what size needles are best to work with, with the yarn you have decided to use. Most yarn labels have printed on them a suggested needle size. Try that first with your pattern and your yarn, and work up a small piece, approximately 3 inches square. If you find the texture of your square too loose, try smaller needles, and if you find it too tight, try larger ones. In spite of the suggested needle size on the label, you may use needles as small or as large as you wish, and your decision should be based only on which needles are most comfortable for you to use with your yarn and which give you the texture you like best. When you have determined this, you are ready to go on to the next step. Measure the 3-inch square of your choice very carefully to determine how many stitches you have to an inch, and how many rows. This will tell you the gauge you are going to work with. Now you go on to the final step in the designing of your afghan.

To give an example, let us say that your little swatch shows you that you are getting 4 stitches and 6 rows to an inch. You already have decided that you are going to make a 60″ x 72″ afghan. The number of stitches per inch on your swatch, multiplied by the width of your finished piece (without fringe or edging), tells you how many stitches you will need to work with: 60 × 4 = 240, so you will be working with approximately 240 stitches. You know that you are using three shades of a color, that you want the deep shade to predominate, and that you should be working your piece in strips for ease in handling. The number of strips you choose to work with and the way in which you divide your colors are completely up to you, depending entirely on how you envision your afghan. Let us assume now, however, again for purposes of example, that you are thinking of something resembling one of the three designs pictured below, any one of which might fit into the general picture you want.

If the afghan you think you would like to make resembles Design No. 1, you would probably be thinking in terms of using perhaps two light strips, two medium strips, and three deep ones. Since you know you want the deep shade to predominate, you might want the deep strips to be wider than the light and medium strips, needing to remember only that the total width of your seven strips must add up to approximately 60 inches, which is the width you have chosen to make your afghan. A good division, in that case, might be the one pictured on Design No. 1—making your light and medium strips each 7 inches wide, your two deep strips at either side of center 10 inches wide, and your center deep strip 12 inches wide. The addition: 7 + 10 + 7 + 12 + 7 + 10 + 7 = 60. Since

A B C B C B A

DESIGN NO. 1

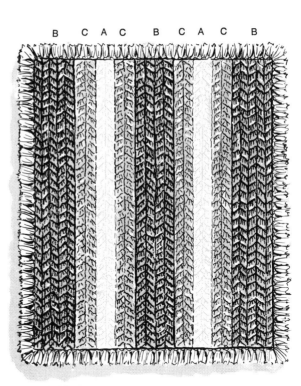

B C A C B C A C B

DESIGN NO. 2

you are using a gauge of 4 stitches to 1 inch, and you need a total of 240 stitches in all, your division and addition would be as follows: $28 + 40 + 28 + 48 + 28 + 40 + 28 = 240$. This then would give you the number of stitches you would be casting on for each of your seven 72-inch-long strips. The stitch you have decided to work with now is a multiple of 4, so your calculations are correct, but if there were a different multiple, you would need now to adjust the number of stitches to the right multiple, and possibly vary the design of your afghan slightly. The following examples show how you might accommodate your design to possible other pattern multiples involved, maintaining the same gauge:

Multiple of 6 stitches: $30 + 36 + 30 + 48 + 30 + 36 + 30 = 240$

Multiple of 8 + 3: $27 + 43 + 27 + 51 + 27 + 43 + 27 = 245$
Multiple of 9 + 1: $28 + 37 + 28 + 55 + 28 + 37 + 28 = 241$
Multiple of 17: $17 + 51 + 17 + 68 + 17 + 51 + 17 = 238$

Any other multiple involved can be worked out and varied in the same manner as those shown above. The differential of an extra inch or two in the width of your afghan can be easily accommodated to the general shape and style of your piece by adding or subtracting an inch or two in the length, if necessary. It should be clear now how you would work out your design, colors, pattern stitch, and gauge to the making of your afghan. We can clarify just a little further by working out Designs No. 2 and No. 3 with you.

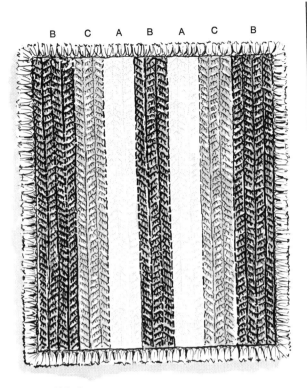

B   C   A   B   A   C   B

DESIGN NO. 3

If you were to be making an afghan like the one illustrated in Design No. 2, you would be making it with nine strips—two of the light color, four medium, and three deep ones—each of your light and medium strips measuring 5 inches and each of your deep ones 10 inches. The addition of your nine strips would be: $10 + 5 + 5 + 5 + 10 + 5 + 5 + 5 + 10 = 60$. Translated into your gauge of 4 stitches to 1 inch, the computation would be $40 + 20 + 20 + 20 + 40 + 20 + 20 + 20 + 40 = 240$. In this instance, we are again assuming a multiple of 4 to your pattern stitch. Should your pattern multiple be different, for example $3 + 1$, your division and addition would be as follows: $37 + 22 + 22 + 22 + 37 + 22 + 22 + 22 + 37 = 243$.

If Design No. 3 is more what you have in mind, you would be making it in seven strips—two light, two

medium, and three deep—the five center strips all the same width, and the two deep ones at either end somewhat wider. Your division of the total width in this case, worked out in inches, would probably be: $10 + 8 + 8 + 8 + 8 + 8 + 10 = 60$. The number of stitches to be cast on for your strips would be $40 + 32 + 32 + 32 + 32 + 32 + 40 = 240$, and if your pattern stitch multiple is 5 instead of 4, then your final number of stitches would be $45 + 30 + 30 + 30 + 30 + 30 + 45 = 240$.

Any of the above examples could easily work out the type of afghan you are thinking of. There are endless variations beyond these, to be worked in the same manner, always involving the simple arithmetic lesson and always adding up to exactly what you want to make. In the way we have worked out together the three afghans illustrated, so you would approach any other design you might have in mind, be it in squares or strips, in one or many colors. The only possible additional variation that might arise would be if you've chosen to make an afghan with an intricate knit-in design; in this case, you would want to use a sheet of graph paper, counting off as many boxes on the paper as the number of stitches you would be using for each strip or square, and filling your pattern into these boxes, so that in knitting you can easily read the graph and copy your design as you go. If you are doing this, and your pattern should be a constant repeat of any number of rows, you would of course need only one repeat on your graph paper to follow and carry on with.

Final finishing of your afghan again becomes a matter of your own choice. You may seam your pieces together, or weave them, or join them with a row of slip stitch or single crochet on either the right or wrong side of your work. Directions for any of these joinings appear in our Knitter's Guide. There are also a wide variety of edgings, including possibly a solid crocheted border, a ruffled or plain chain loop edge, or fringe involving either a plain or fancy knotting pattern. Check the paragraphs on afghans in our Designer's Guide for suggestions on edgings, then, using self- or contrast-color yarn for whichever edging you choose, finish your piece, block it carefully according to directions in the Knitter's Guide, and enjoy it!

To discuss a little further now the art of designing, let us assume that you want to make a sweater for yourself, perhaps the first you've ever made, or perhaps one of many others you've made before. You are a Size 12 and you want your sweater to be a little different. You want it quite long, and you want a hem at the bottom instead of the traditional ribbing. You want it to be nipped at the waist with about a 5-inch knit 1, purl 1 mini-rib waistline, and to have a ribbed turtleneck and long sleeves with exaggerated ribbed cuffs. You would like to use a small all-over textured stitch for all portions except those that are ribbed. You are probably thinking in terms of a garment like the one pictured in Design No. 4. How do you start?

Choose your yarn, again with the assurance, as already discussed, that you will have enough of the dye lot involved to complete your garment. Select the pattern stitch that you want, then swatch it out to determine the needle size you want to use. Measure your gauge, note the multiple of the pattern stitch you have selected, then consult the standard size chart in the Knitter's Guide in Chapter 7. Measure your body proportions to be certain that your own measurements conform to those on the standard size chart. Wherever there is a variation, you must in those parts substitute your own measurements for those on the chart. Assuming, however, that your measurements do conform and that you have selected a pattern stitch with a multiple of 3, and a gauge of 5 stitches and 7 rows to an inch using No. 9 needles, you would proceed with your calculations much as you did in designing one of the afghans. You would need, however, to take into consideration, in the designing of a garment, the additional mathematics involved in the various shapings, such as armholes, neck, and sleeves.

DESIGN NO. 4

STANDARD MEASUREMENTS FOR
A WOMAN'S SIZE 12:

Bust	34″	Armhole depth 7¼″
Waist	25″	Waist to
Shoulder back	13″	underarm 8″
Shoulder	4¼″	Underarm
Back of neck	4½″	sleeve length 18″
		Sleeve width
		at underarm 12″

For most garments, one works the back first, the front, or fronts if the garment is a cardigan-type, next, and the sleeves last before final finishing of sewing seams and adding details such as neckbands, collars, pockets, and other trim. For slipovers the number of stitches is the same on both back and front, and that number of stitches is usually the number involved in the calculation of the bust or chest measurement, divided in half. To determine the number of stitches for the back and front of the slipover you are making, divide your bust measurement in half: 34″ divided by 2 = 17″. 17 × 5 (your gauge) = 85. Since 85 is not divisible by your pattern stitch multiple of 3, you must use either 84 or 87 stitches. Generally it is better to use the larger number of stitches, since this can only add more comfort to the fit of your garment. Your next addition would be that of approximately ½ inch to each piece for the allowance of seaming. 87 + 3 = 90. This becomes the number of stitches you will cast on for the back of your sweater.

You want a hemline at the bottom, and let's assume, for purposes of illustration, that you want your sweater to measure 16 inches from the hemmed bottom to your underarm. You will find complete directions for forming hemlines in our Knitter's Guide, but for now it is enough to know that an extra inch is usually added to the length of your garment for hemming and that it is most often worked on needles three sizes smaller than those used for the rest of your sweater, and in stockinette stitch (knit 1 row, purl 1 row), regardless of any pattern stitch used elsewhere in the garment. The ribbed portions you are using are also usually worked on needles three sizes smaller. The measurement from your waist to your underarm is, according to the chart, 8 inches. Since you want a 5-inch ribbed waistline, you would probably want, for good proportion, that part of your sweater to extend from 2 inches below the waistline to 3 inches above. Average ribbed cuffs on ladies' sweaters measure between 2 and 2½ inches, and since you want an exaggerated cuff, you would probably want to have it measure 5 inches, which would balance well with your ribbed waistline. Assuming now that the differential of your sleeve from its narrowest portion at the wrist to its measurement of 12 inches at the widest underarm portion is 4 inches, you will need to plan on increasing those 4 inches in the working of the sleeve. Sleeve increasing is usually done at gradual intervals at either end of the needle after the ribbing is completed. Round neck shaping at the front usually begins 2 inches below the

shoulders, and turtlenecks average between 4 and 5 inches in length, which makes them just half that width when turned over. Keeping the above information in mind—and referring to our Knitter's Guide for all techniques such as decreasing and binding off and picking up stitches around the neck, and to our Designer's Guide for such information as neck, shoulder, and sleeve shaping—you would work your sweater in the following manner:

Back: With No. 6 needles, cast on 90 stitches. Work in stockinette stitch for 1 inch, then form hemline (see our Knitter's Guide). Change now to No. 9 needles and pattern stitch, and work even until piece measures 6 inches above hemline. Change to No. 6 needles and knit 1, purl 1 ribbing, and work even in ribbing for 5 inches. Change again to No. 9 needles and pattern stitch, and work for 5 inches more, ending with a wrong side row. **Shape Armholes:** At beginning of each of the next 2 rows bind off 5 stitches, then decrease 1 stitch at beginning and end of every other row 6 times. Work even now on 68 stitches until piece measures 7¼ inches above start of armhole shaping, ending with a wrong side row. **Shape Shoulders:** At beginning of each of the next 4 rows bind off 11 stitches. Bind off loosely remaining 24 stitches for back of neck. **Front:** Work same as for Back until piece measures 5¼ inches above start of armhole shaping, ending with a wrong side row. **Shape Neck:** Work across 25 stitches, join another ball of yarn, bind off center 18 stitches, then work across remaining 25 stitches. Continuing to maintain pattern stitch as established and working on both sides at once, at each neck edge decrease 1 stitch every other row 3 times. Work even now on 22 stitches of each side until piece measures same as Back to start of shoulder shaping, ending with a wrong side row. Shape shoulders as on Back. **Sleeves:** With No. 6 needles cast on 42 stitches. Work even in knit 1, purl 1 ribbing until piece measures 5 inches in all. Change to No. 9 needles and pattern stitch, and work even for

1 inch, then increase 1 stitch at beginning and end of next row, and repeat this increase every 1 inch until there are 62 stitches in all, adding more patterns as stitches are increased. Work even now on 62 stitches until piece measures 18 inches in all, or desired length to underarm, ending with a wrong side row, then **Shape Cap:** Bind off 5 stitches at beginning of each of the next 2 rows, then decrease 1 stitch at beginning and end of every other row for 4¼ inches. (Note: This figure for length in shaping the sleeve cap is always 3 inches less than the total armhole length, as shown in our Designer's Guide.) Bind off 3 stitches at the beginning of each of the next 4 rows. (Note: Usually a maximum of 2 inches is left for the final sleeve bind-off, also described in our Designer's Guide.) Bind off remaining stitches. **Finishing:** Sew side, sleeve, and shoulder seams, working a thin seam with an overhand back stitch. The choice of other methods of seaming appears in our Knitter's Guide. **Turtleneck:** With round No. 6 needle, and right side of work facing, pick up and knit all stitches around neck. Join, and working around, knit 1, purl 1 in ribbing for 5 inches. Bind off loosely in ribbing. Block sweater with a warm iron over a damp cloth.

Once more now, for purposes of illustration, let us work out another design together. You want to make a man's double-breasted V-necked cardigan jacket. You want to make it in a medium size (40–42) and in a fairly loose ribbed pattern stitch, and you'd like it to have a patch pocket on either side of the bottom, a smaller one on the upper left side, and a contrast-color crocheted edging around the front, neck, and pockets. Again, you are probably thinking in terms of a garment like the one pictured in Design No. 5.

The measurements shown above seem to conform to the size you want to make. However, in designing looser fitting garments such as jackets or coats, you usually allow for an extra inch in width on back, front, and sleeves for ease of fit, and you also take into consideration the fact that armholes

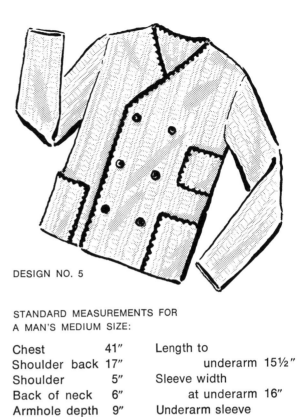

DESIGN NO. 5

STANDARD MEASUREMENTS FOR
A MAN'S MEDIUM SIZE:

Chest	41"	Length to	
Shoulder back	17"		underarm 15½"
Shoulder	5"	Sleeve width	
Back of neck	6"		at underarm 16"
Armhole depth	9"	Underarm sleeve	
			length 19¼"

are a little deeper and sleeves are usually less tapered at the bottom. The rib pattern stitch you have chosen is a multiple of 2, and your gauge is 4 stitches and 6 rows to 1 inch. Your design mathematics would work in the following manner:

The chest measurement you are using is 41 inches. Divided in half, this becomes 20½ inches for the back of your jacket, plus 1 inch for ease, plus ½ inch for seam allowance. Your back, then, would need to measure 22 inches. The front of a slipover usually starts with the same number of stitches as the back. On any cardigan type of garment, however, as we've mentioned before, that number of stitches is divided in half again, one part for the right front, and one for the left—and extra stitches are added to each part for the center overlap, this being the number of stitches you are planning for the width of the overlap. In this instance your back measures 22 inches, so each front would be 11 inches in order to meet right at center; but since you are having probably a 6-inch overlap (this seems to be good proportion for a double-breasted overlap on the size of jacket you are making), you would need to add 3 inches more onto each front to accommodate the overlap. This would make the size of each of your fronts 14 inches.

Your sleeve width measurement for the size you are making is 16 inches at the underarm, which is its widest part, and here again you will add something for ease, perhaps ½ inch on a sleeve and an additional ½ inch for seam allowance. This makes your sleeve 17 inches at its widest part. Since it is a jacket you are making, you do not want a tight-fitting tapered sleeve, so you will allow only 2 inches for the difference in width between the narrowest and widest parts, remembering that you are not using ribbing at the bottom of the sleeves to hold and shape them. The sleeves, then, would begin with a measurement of 15 inches.

The larger pockets will probably proportion right to 5 inches square, without edging, and the smaller one to 3 inches square, and most likely you will want three sets of double buttons, the first set occurring 4 inches above the bottom and the last 1 inch below the start of the V-neck shaping. Again, referring to Chapter 8 for all techniques and design principles, you would probably design your jacket as follows:

Back: Cast on 88 stitches. Work even in pattern until piece measures 15½ inches, or desired length to underarm, ending with a wrong side row. **Shape armholes:** At beginning of each of the next 2 rows bind off 5 stitches, then decrease 1 stitch at beginning and end of every other row 7 times. Work even now on 64 stitches until piece measures 9½ inches above start of armhole shaping, ending with a

wrong side row. **Shape shoulders:** At beginning of each of the next 4 rows bind off 10 stitches. Bind off loosely remaining 24 stitches for back of neck. **Right front:** (Note: In any cardigan type of garment, the side without buttonholes is worked first.) Cast on 56 stitches. Work even in pattern until piece measures 15 inches from start, ending at front edge. **Shape V-neck:** At beginning of the next row decrease 1 stitch and repeat the decrease every other row 23 times more, and *at same time* when piece measures the same as Back to armhole, ending at side edge, shape armhole as on Back. When 20 stitches remain, work even until piece measures same as Back to shoulder, ending at side edge. Shape shoulder as on Back. **Left front:** Work same as Right Front, reversing all shaping, and working in three sets of double buttonholes, the first set 4 inches from start, the last set 1 inch below start of neck shaping, and the remaining set spaced evenly between. **To make double buttonholes:** Starting at front edge, work across 4 stitches, bind off 2 stitches, work across 12 stitches, bind off next 2 stitches, work to end of row. On return row, cast on 2 stitches over each set of 2 bound-off stitches on previous row. **Sleeves:** Cast on 62 stitches. Work even in pattern until piece measures 3 inches. Increase 1 stitch at beginning and end of next row, and repeat this increase every 3½ inches 3 times more. Work even now on 70 stitches until piece measures 19¼ inches, or desired length to underarm. **Shape cap:** At beginning of the next 2 rows, bind off 5 stitches, then decrease 1 stitch at beginning and end of every other row for 6½ inches. At beginning of each of the next 4 rows, bind off 3 stitches. Bind off remaining stitches. **Finishing:** Sew side, sleeve, and shoulder seams. Sew in sleeves. **Large pockets** (Make two): Cast on 20 stitches. Work even in pattern for 5 inches. Bind off loosely. **Small pocket:** Cast on 16 stitches. Work even in pattern for 4 inches. Work 1 row self-color single crochet around all outer edges of jacket, and around four sides of each pocket, working 3 single crochet in each corner stitch as you turn. Work 1 row contrast-color single crochet around front, neck, and pocket edges. Sew pockets in place as desired. Sew on buttons to correspond to buttonholes. Block jacket with a warm iron over a damp cloth.

We hope that a good knowledge of the art of designing knitwear has been imparted to you in this chapter, that you feel happy about having learned a new creative skill, and are stimulated to go on to enjoy many pleasant leisure hours. The same starting choice of a style or pattern and yarn and needles and gauge, and the same rudimentary mathematics, combined with the information in our Knitter's Guide and Designer's Guide, all add up to everything that you need to know in order to design and make anything you want. You can create a brand-new design, or work out something you've seen to your own dimensions, or copy one of your favorite pieces of clothing and adapt it to knitwear, or even buy an attractive sewing pattern, measure off the tissues enclosed, exercise simple mathematics, and reproduce it as a beautifully fitting and completely original knitted garment. We hope you will have found a new avenue of release for personal expression, and even perhaps for some latent talent that, unknown to yourself, may have been bottled up within you for years.

6

Pattern stitches

Photographed here are some three hundred different pattern stitches, any one of which you might want to select for use in your own designs, or to substitute for other patterns in designs you have seen elsewhere. Some of the stitches are quite simple to work, others more intricate. By and large, the stitches are categorized, starting with vertical, diagonal, and horizontal ribbings, then going on to richly textured stitches, to gossamer, lacy patterns, interesting cable twists, and finally to patterns involving more than one color. Directions are given for making all of the stitches shown, and your own choice of which you use can alter completely the look of whatever it is you are making. A tailored sweater with a simple texture can metamorphose into a delicate, sheer creation with the use of one of the lacy stitches. Your imagination at this point has completely free rein, and though certain stitches are perhaps more suitable to particular types of garments, still the choice of the one you use is entirely your own, and up to the dictates of your own good taste.

Of all the stitches shown here, the most basic ones, used in practically every pattern, are the knit stitch and the purl stitch. Illustrations of how to do these two basic stitches appear in our Knitter's Guide in Chapter 7. Shown on p. 20, uncategorized by virtue of being so basic, are the garter stitch (knit each row), the stockinette stitch (1 row knit and 1 row purl), and the knit 1, purl 1 ribbing, where a knit and purl stitch alternate throughout to form the ribbed pattern. Also directly below is an explanation of the various abbreviations used in each pattern, and a definition of the word "multiple," which appears in each set of directions, and of three instruction details appearing in many patterns below and causing a difference in the look of the pattern if they are done in any manner other than that described. In the making of our two-color patterns, we used a light color for the main color and a deeper one for the contrast color. In our three-color patterns, we used a light color for **A**, a medium color for **B**, and a deep color for **C**. If other color gradations are used, they may be equally attractive but will show some variation in the appearance of the pattern.

ABBREVIATIONS

Beginning	beg
Contrast color	CC
Decrease	dec
Double point	dp
Increase	inc
Knit	k
Loop	lp
Main color	MC
Pass slip stitch over	psso
Pattern	pat
Purl	p
Repeat	rep
Skip	sk
Slip stitch	sl st
Stitch	st
Together	tog
Yarn over	yo

A **stitch multiple** is that number of stitches necessary to complete one pattern. The number of stitches you use in your work needs to be divisible by the number of the original multiple. Example: A pattern with a multiple of 4 must be worked on a number of stitches divisible by 4, such as 8, 12, 16, or any other multiple of the original 4. The variation where a multiple has an additional figure at the end, such as 4 + 1, means that the number of stitches needs again to be divisible by the original number multiple with 1 extra stitch added just at the end. In this case the number of stitches used might be 9, 13, 17, or any other multiple of 4 + 1.

K the p sts and p the k sts of previous row means to knit all stitches with the loop in back (this loop is actually the top of the stitch on previous row), and purl all the stitches with the loop in front.

K the 2nd st on left needle, k the 1st st, and drop both sts from left needle means to knit the 2nd stitch from right to left through the back of stitch and knit the 1st stitch from left to right through the front of stitch.

Sl st as if to k when the previous stitch is a purl stitch means to bring yarn to back of work before transferring it from left to right needle. **Sl st as if to p** when the previous stitch is a knit stitch means to bring yarn to front of work before transferring it.

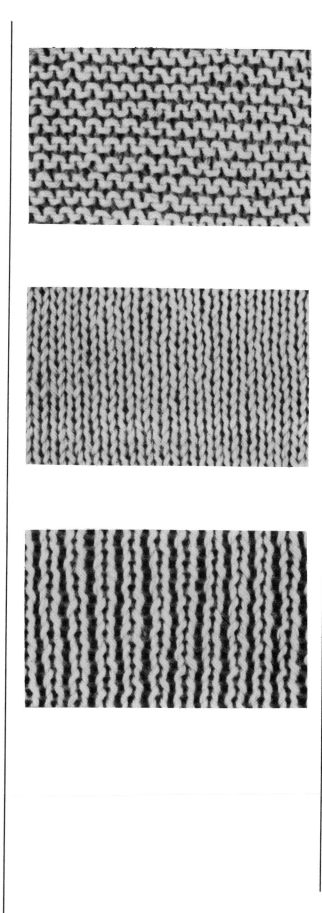

The garter stitch

Multiple of any number of sts: **Row 1:** K. Repeat this row for pattern.

The stockinette stitch

Multiple of any number of sts: **Row 1:** K. **Row 2:** P.

The knit 1, purl 1 rib

Multiple of any even number of sts: **Row 1:** * K 1, p 1, repeat from * across. Repeat this row for pattern.

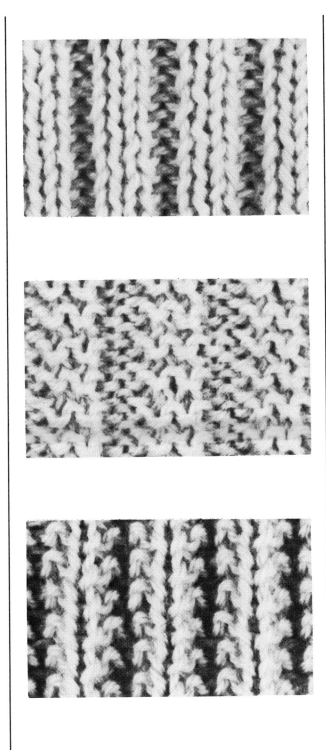

[1]
Multiple of 2 sts: **Row 1:** * K 2, p 2, repeat from * across.
Row 2: K the p sts and p the k sts of previous row.

[2]
Multiple of 2 sts: **Row 1:** * K 2, p 2, repeat from * across.
Row 2: K.

[3]
Multiple of 4 sts: **Row 1:** * K 3, p 1, repeat from * across.
Row 2: * K 2, p 1, k 1, repeat from * across.

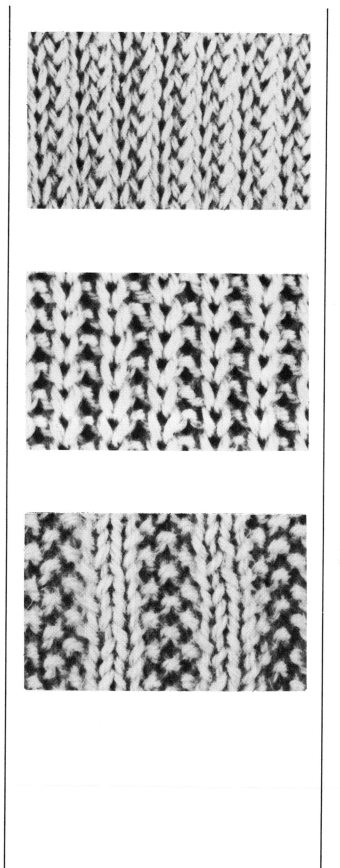

[4]
Multiple of 2 sts: **Row 1:** * K 1, sl 1, repeat from * across.
Row 2: * P 1, sl 1, repeat from * across.

[5]
Multiple of 2 sts plus 1: **Row 1:** P 1, * sl 1 as if to k, p 1,
repeat from * across. **Row 2:** P.

[6]
Multiple of 5 sts plus 2: **Row 1:** * K 2, p 1, k 1, p 1,
repeat from * across and end k 2. **Row 2:** P 3, * k 1, p 4,
repeat from * across, and end p 3.

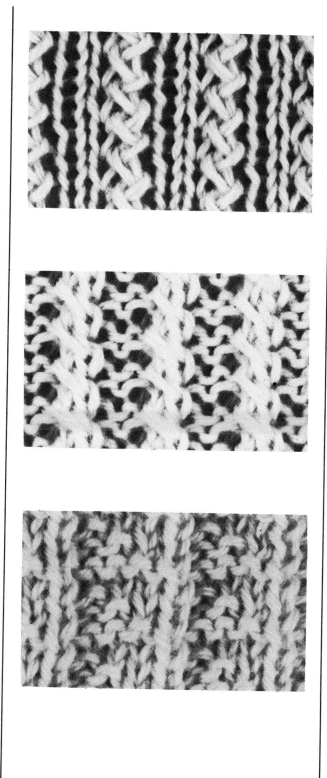

[7]
Multiple of 4 sts plus 2: **Row 1:** * K 2, k the 2nd st on left-hand needle, k the 1st st, and drop both sts from left-hand needle, repeat from * across, and end k 2.
Row 2: * P 2, p the 2nd st on left-hand needle, p the 1st st, drop both sts from left-hand needle, repeat from * across, and end p 2.

[8]
Multiple of 4 sts plus 2: **Row 1 (wrong side):** K 2, * p 2, k 2, repeat from * across. **Row 2:** P 2, * k the 2nd st on left-hand needle, k the 1st st, and drop both sts from left-hand needle, p 2, repeat from * across.

[9]
Multiple of 5 sts: **Rows 1 and 4:** * K 1, p 4, repeat from * across. **Rows 2 and 3:** * K 3, p 2, repeat from * across.

[10]
Multiple of 7 sts: **Rows 1 and 3:** * P 2, k 1, p 2, k 2, repeat from * across. **Row 2:** * P 2, k 2, p 1, k 2, repeat from * across. **Row 4:** K.

[11]
Multiple of 4 sts plus 2: **Row 1:** * K 2, sl 2 as if to p, repeat from * across, and end k 2. **Row 2:** P.

[12]
Multiple of 5 sts: **Row 1:** * P 2, k 1, sl 1, k 1, repeat from * across. **Row 2:** * P 3, k 2, repeat from * across.

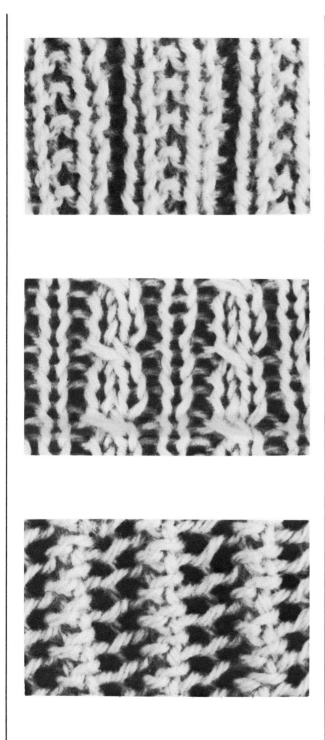

[13]
Multiple of 5 sts plus 2: **Row 1:** * P 2, k 1, p 1, k 1, repeat from * across, and end p 2. **Row 2:** * K 2, p 3, repeat from * across, and end k 2.

[14]
Multiple of 5 sts: **Row 1:** * K 1, p 1, k 2, p 1, repeat from * across. **Rows 2 and 4:** * K 1, p 2, k 1, p 1, repeat from * across. **Row 3:** * K 1, p 1, k the 2nd st on left-hand needle, k the 1st st, and drop both sts from left-hand needle, p 1, repeat from * across.

[15]
Multiple of 3 sts plus 1: **Row 1:** K 2, yo, * k 2 tog, k 1, yo, repeat from * across, and end k 2 tog. Repeat this row for pattern.

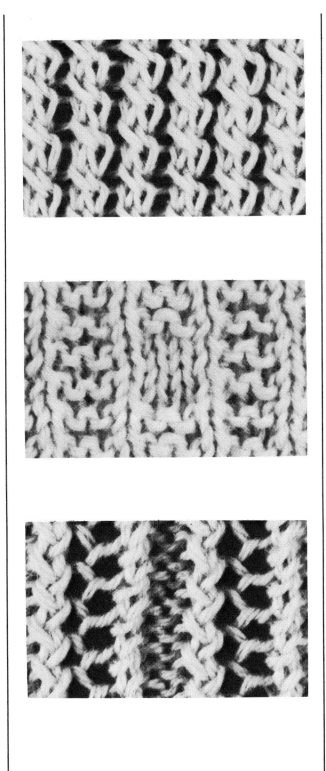

[16]
Multiple of 2 sts: **Row 1:** * K the 2nd st on left-hand needle, k the 1st st, and drop both sts from left-hand needle, repeat from * across. **Row 2:** P.

[17]
Multiple of 6 sts: **Rows 1 and 3:** * P 2, k 4, repeat from * across. **Rows 2, 4, 6, and 8:** P. **Rows 5 and 7:** K 3, * p 2, k 1, repeat from * across, and end p 2, k 1.

[18]
Multiple of 6 sts: **Row 1:** * P 2, k 2 tog, yo, k 2, repeat from * across. **Row 2:** * P 2 tog, yo, p 2, k 2, repeat from * across.

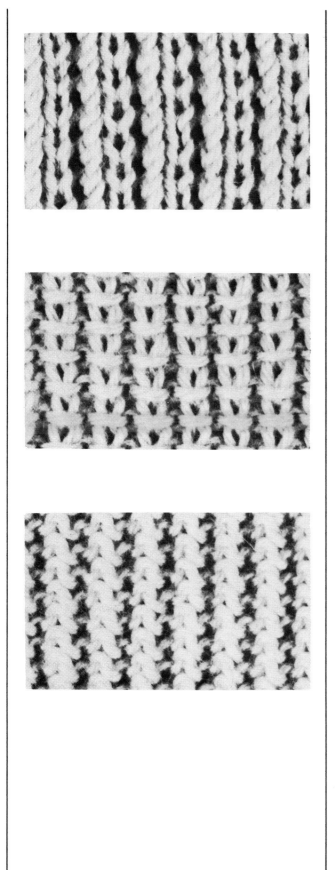

[19]
Multiple of 2 sts: **Row 1:** * K 1, sl 1 as if to p, yo, repeat from * across, and end k 2. **Row 2:** P 2, * p 2 tog, **p 1,** repeat from * across.

[20]
Multiple of 2 sts: **Row 1:** P 2, * sl 1, p 1, repeat from * across. **Row 2:** * K 1, p 1, repeat from * across.

[21]
Multiple of 2 sts plus 1: **Row 1:** K 1, * sl 1, k 1, repeat from * across. **Row 2:** K.

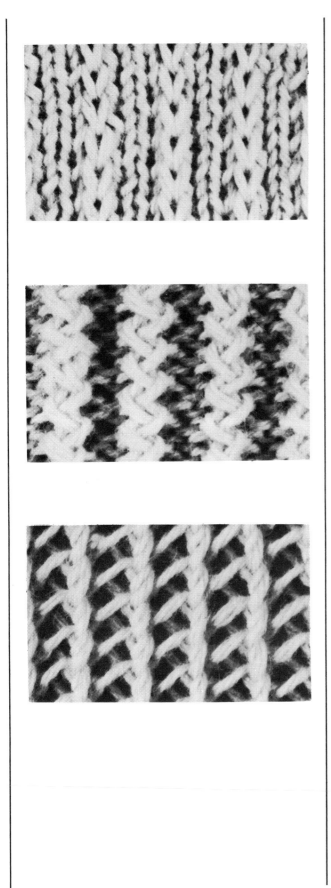

[22]
Multiple of 3 sts plus 1: **Row 1:** K 1, * sl 1, k 2, repeat from * across. **Row 2:** P.

[23]
Multiple of 4 sts plus 2: **Row 1:** P 2, * k into back of 2nd st on left-hand needle, k the 1st st, and drop both sts from left-hand needle, p 2, repeat from * across. **Row 2:** K 2, * p the 2nd st on left-hand needle, p the 1st st, and drop both sts from left-hand needle, k 2, repeat from * across.

[24]
Multiple of 2 sts: **Row 1:** * Yo, sl 1 as if to p, k 1, repeat from * across. **Row 2:** * Yo, sl 1 as if to p, k 2 tog, repeat from * across. Repeat Row 2 for pattern.

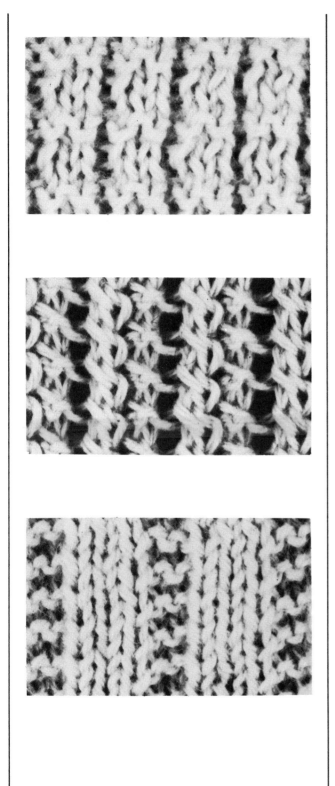

[25]
Multiple of 3 sts: **Rows 1 and 3:** * K 2, p 1, repeat from * across. **Row 2:** * K 1, p 2, repeat from * across. **Row 4:** K.

[26]
Multiple of 4 sts plus 2: **Row 1 (wrong side):** K 2, * p 2, k 2, repeat from * across. **Row 2:** * K the 2nd st on left-hand needle, k the 1st st, and drop both sts from left-hand needle, repeat from * across.

[27]
Multiple of 5 sts plus 3: **Row 1:** K. **Row 2:** * P 3, k 2, repeat from * across, and end p 3.

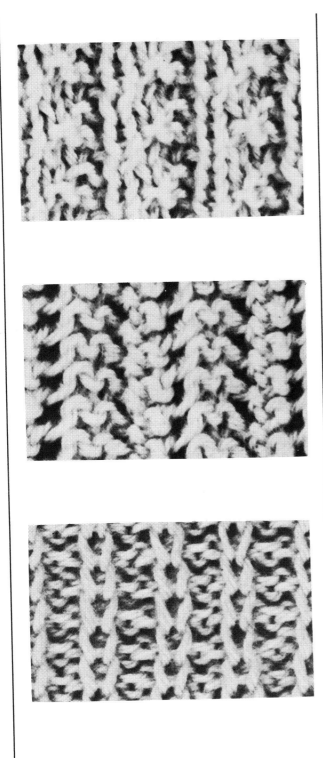

[28]
Multiple of 4 sts plus 1: **Row 1:** K 1, * p 3, k 1, repeat from * across. **Row 2:** * P 2, k 2, repeat from * across, and end p 1. **Row 3:** K 1, * p 1, k 3, repeat from * across. **Row 4:** P.

[29]
Multiple of 4 sts plus 2: **Row 1:** K 2, * yo loosely, k 2, pass yo over the 2 sts just worked, k 2, repeat from * across. Repeat this row for pattern.

[30]
Multiple of 3 sts plus 2: **Row 1:** P 2, * sl 1 as if to k, p 2, repeat from * across. **Row 2:** K 2, * p 1, k 2, repeat from * across.

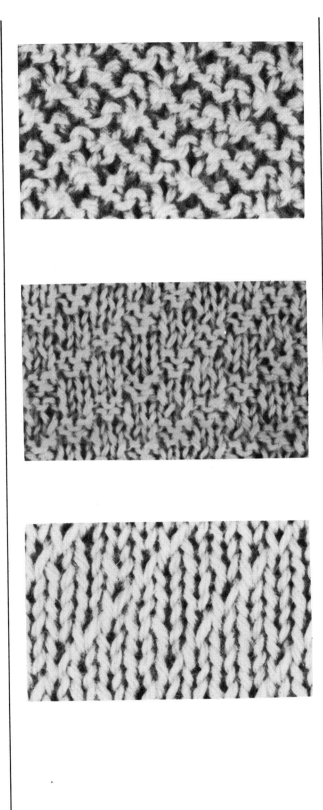

[31]

Multiple of 4 sts: **Row 1:** * K 2, p 2, repeat from * across. **Rows 2, 4, 6, and 8:** K the k sts and p the p sts of previous row. **Row 3:** * K 1, p 2, k 1, repeat from * across. **Row 5:** * P 2, k 2, repeat from * across. **Row 7:** * P 1, k 2, p 1, repeat from * across.

[32]

Multiple of 6 sts: **Row 1:** * K 4, p 2, repeat from * across. **Rows 2, 4, and 6:** K the p sts and p the k sts of previous row. **Row 3:** * K 2, p 2, k 2, repeat from * across. **Row 5:** * P 2, k 4, repeat from * across.

[33]

Multiple of 4 sts: **Row 1:** * K 3, sl 1, repeat from * across. **Rows 2, 4, 6, and 8:** P. **Row 3:** * K 2, sl 1, K 1, repeat from * across. **Row 5:** * K 1, sl 1, k 2, repeat from * across. **Row 7:** * Sl 1, k 3, repeat from * across.

[34]
Multiple of 6 sts: **Rows 1, 2, and 3:** * K 3, p 3, repeat from * across. **Rows 4 and 6:** * P 1, k 3, p 2, repeat from * across. **Rows 5, 8, 14, and 17:** K the p sts and p the k sts of previous row. **Rows 7 and 9:** * K 1, p 3, k 2, repeat from * across. **Rows 10, 11, and 12:** * P 3, k 3, repeat from * across. **Rows 13 and 15:** * P 2, k 3, p 1, repeat from * across. **Rows 16 and 18:** * K 2, p 3, k 1, repeat from * across.

[35]
Multiple of 2 sts: **Row 1:** * Sl 1 as if to p, k 1, yo, psso the yo and the k 1, repeat from * across. **Rows 2 and 4:** P. **Row 3:** K 1, * sl 1 as if to p, k 1, yo, psso the k 1 and the yo, repeat from * across, and end k 1.

[36]
Multiple of 4 sts: **Row 1:** * K 2, p 2, repeat from * across. **Rows 2, 4, 6, and 8:** P. **Row 3:** K 1, * p 2, k 2, repeat from * across, and end k 1. **Row 5:** * P 2, k 2, repeat from * across. **Row 7:** P 1, * k 2, p 2, repeat from * across, and end p 1.

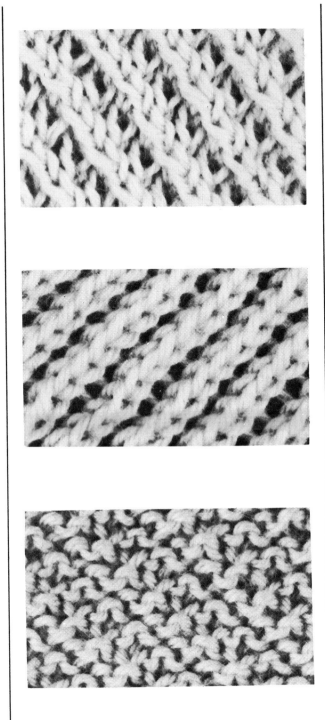

[37]
Multiple of 3 sts: **Row 1:** * K in back lp of 2nd st on left-hand needle, k the 1st st, drop both sts from left-hand needle (left twist), k 1, repeat from * across. **Rows 2, 4, and 6:** P. **Row 3:** K 1, * left twist on next 2 sts, k 1, repeat from * across, and end left twist. **Row 5:** K 2, * left twist on next 2 sts, k 1, repeat from * across, and end k 1.

[38]
Multiple of 2 sts: **Row 1:** K. **Row 2:** P 1, * yo, p 2 tog, repeat from * across, and end p 1. **Row 3:** K 2, * yo, k 2 tog, repeat from * across. **Row 4:** P 2, * yo, p 2 tog, repeat from * across. **Row 5:** K 1, * yo, k 2 tog, repeat from * across, and end k 1. Repeat Rows 2 through 5 for pattern.

[39]
Multiple of 4 sts: **Row 1:** * K 2, p 2, repeat from * across. **Rows 2, 4, 6, and 8:** K the k sts and p the p sts of previous row. **Row 3:** P 1, * k 2, p 2, repeat from * across, and end p 1. **Row 5:** P 2, * k 2, p 2, repeat from * across, and end k 2. **Row 7:** K 1, p 2, * k 2, p 2, repeat from * across, and end k 1.

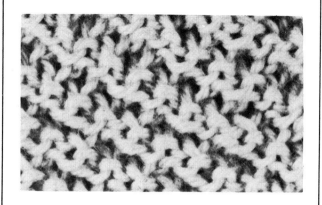

[40]
Multiple of 4 sts: **Row 1:** * K 2, p 2, repeat from * across. **Row 2:** * K 1, p 2, k 1, repeat from * across. **Row 3:** * P 2, k 2, repeat from * across. **Row 4:** * P 1, k 2, p 1, repeat from * across.

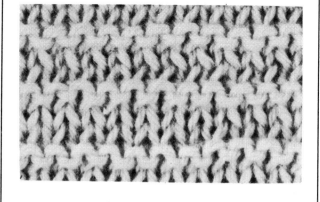

[41]
Multiple of any number of sts: **Rows 1, 3, and 4:** K. **Row 2:** P.

[42]
Multiple of any number of sts: **Rows 1, 3, 4, and 6:** K. **Rows 2 and 5:** P.

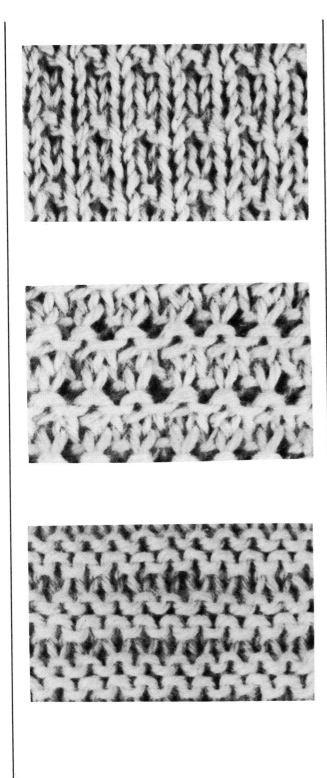

[43]
Multiple of 2 sts: **Row 1:** K. **Rows 2 and 4:** P. **Row 3:** * K 1, p 1, repeat from * across.

[44]
Multiple of 2 sts: **Row 1:** K. **Row 2:** K 2 tog across. **Row 3:** K into front and back of each st. **Row 4:** P.

[45]
Multiple of any number of sts: **Rows 1 and 4:** K. **Rows 2 and 3:** P.

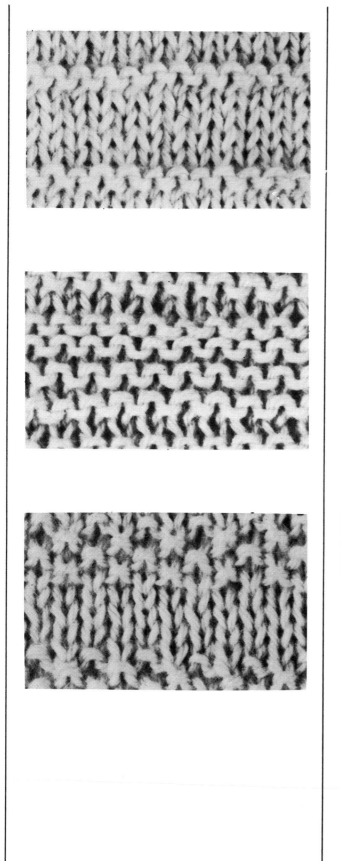

[46]
Multiple of 2 sts: **Rows 1, 3, 5, and 6: K. Rows 2 and 4: P.**

[47]
Multiple of any number of sts: **Rows 1, 2, 3, 4, 5, and 6: K. Rows 7 and 8: P.**

[48]
Multiple of any number of sts: **Rows 1 and 3: K. Rows 2 and 4: P. Rows 5 and 7: * K 1, p 1, repeat from * across. Rows 6 and 8:** K the k sts and p the p sts of previous row.

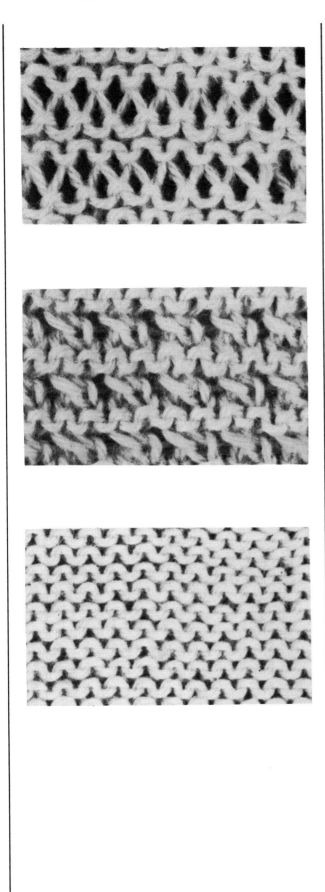

[49]
Multiple of any number of sts: **Rows 1 and 2:** K. **Row 3:** K 1, * yo, k 1, repeat from * across. **Row 4:** K, dropping yo's of previous row.

[50]
Multiple of 2 sts: **Row 1:** * K the 2nd st on left-hand needle, k the 1st st and drop both sts from left-hand needle, repeat from * across. **Rows 2 and 3:** K. **Row 4:** P.

[51]
Multiple of any number of sts: **Row 1 (right side):** P. **Row 2:** K.

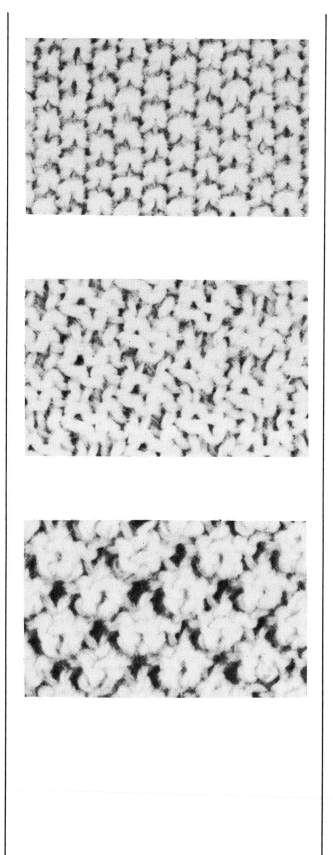

[52]
Multiple of 2 sts plus 1: **Row 1:** * K 1, p 1, repeat from * across, and end k 1. Repeat this row for pattern.

[53]
Multiple of 4 sts: **Rows 1 and 2:** * K 2, p 2, repeat from * across. **Rows 3 and 4:** * P 2, k 2, repeat from * across.

[54]
Multiple of 4 sts: **Rows 1 and 3 (right side):** P. **Row 2:** * (K 1, p 1, k 1) in next st, p next 3 sts tog, repeat from * across. **Row 4:** * P 3 tog, (k 1, p 1, k 1) in next st, repeat from * across.

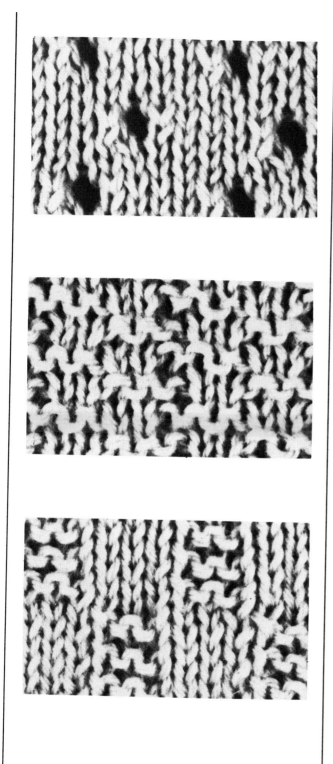

[55]
Multiple of 6 sts: **Row 1:** K. **Rows 2, 4, 6, and 8:** P.
Row 3: * K 4, yo, k 2 tog, repeat from * across. **Row 5:**
K. **Row 7:** K 2, * yo, k 2 tog, k 4, repeat from * across,
and end k 2.

[56]
Multiple of 5 sts: **Row 1:** * P 3, k 2, repeat from * across.
Rows 2 and 4: P. **Row 3:** * P 1, k 2, p 2, repeat from *
across.

[57]
Multiple of 6 sts plus 4: **Rows 1, 3, and 5:** * K 4, p 2,
repeat from * across, and end k 4. **Rows 2, 4, 6, 8, 10,
and 12:** P. **Rows 7, 9, and 11:** K 1, * p 2, k 4, repeat
from * across, and end p 2, k 1.

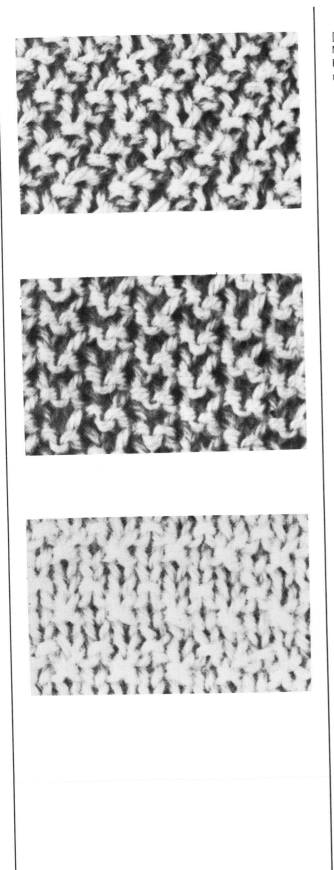

[58]
Multiple of 2 sts: **Row 1:** * K 1, p 1, repeat from * across.
Rows 2 and 4: K the k sts and p the p sts of previous
row. **Row 3:** * P 1, k 1, repeat from * across.

[59]
Multiple of 4 sts: **Row 1:** * K 2, sl 2, repeat from * across.
Row 2: * P 2, k 2, repeat from * across. **Row 3:** * Sl 2,
k 2, repeat from * across. **Row 4:** * K 2, p 2, repeat from
* across.

[60]
Multiple of 2 sts plus 1: **Rows 1 and 2:** * K 1, p 1, repeat
from * across, and end k 1. **Row 3:** K. **Row 4:** P.

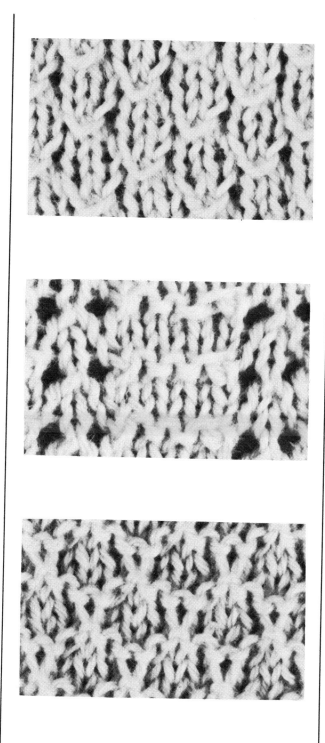

[61]
Multiple of 4 sts: **Rows 1 and 3**: K. **Row 2**: * Yo, p 2, pass yo over the p 2, p 2, repeat from * across. **Row 4**: * P 2, yo, p 2, pass yo over the p 2, repeat from * across.

[62]
Multiple of 7 sts: **Row 1:** * P 1, p 2 tog, yo, p 1, yo, p 2 tog, p 1, repeat from * across. **Rows 2 and 4:** P. **Row 3:** K.

[63]
Multiple of 4 sts: **Rows 1 and 3:** * K 3, sl 1, repeat from * across. **Row 2:** * Sl 1, p 3, repeat from * across. **Rows 4 and 8:** K. **Rows 5 and 7:** * K 1, sl 1, k 2, repeat from * across. **Row 6:** * P 2, sl 1, p 1, repeat from * across.

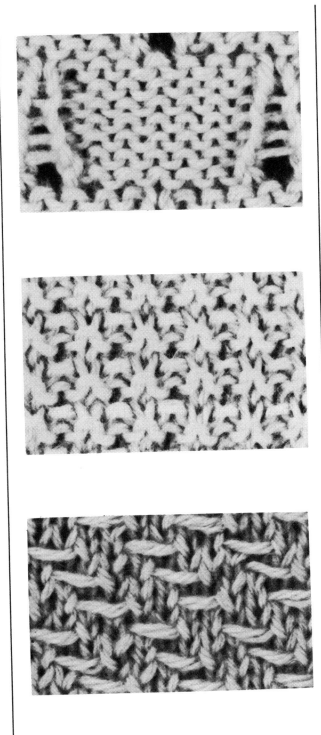

[64]
Multiple of 8 sts: **Row 1:** * Yo, p 2 tog, p 6, repeat from *
across. **Rows 2, 4, and 6:** * K 7, p 1, repeat from *
across. **Rows 3, 5, and 7:** * K 1, p 7, repeat from *
across. **Rows 8 and 16:** P. **Row 9:** * P 4, yo, p 2 tog,
p 2, repeat from * across. **Rows 10, 12, and 14:** * K 3,
p 1, k 4, repeat from * across. **Rows 11, 13, and 15:** * P 4,
k 1, p 3, repeat from * across.

[65]
Multiple of 2 sts plus 1: **Row 1 (wrong side):** K. **Row 2:**
K 1, * sl 1, k 1, repeat from * across. **Row 3:** K 1, * sl 1
as if to p, k 1, repeat from * across. **Row 4:** K.

[66]
Multiple of 4 sts plus 2: **Row 1:** * K 2, sl 2 as if to p,
repeat from * across, and end k 2. **Rows 2, 4 and 6:** P.
Row 3: Sl 1 as if to p, * k 2, sl 2 as if to p, repeat from *
across, and end k 1. **Row 5:** Sl 2 as if to p, * k 2, sl 2 as
if to p, repeat from * across.

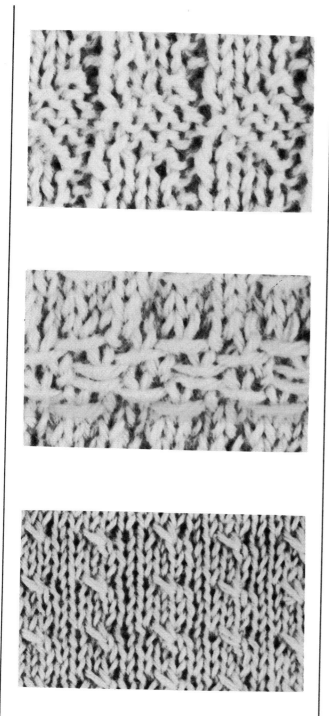

[67]
Multiple of 4 sts: **Row 1:** P. **Rows 2 and 8:** * P 1, k 3, repeat from * across. **Rows 3 and 7:** * P 2, k 2, repeat from * across. **Rows 4 and 6:** * P 3, k 1, repeat from * across. **Row 5:** K.

[68]
Multiple of 10 sts: **Rows 1 and 11:** * K 1, sl 3 as if to p, k 2, sl 3 as if to p, k 1, repeat from * across. **Rows 2 and 10:** * Sl 3, p 2, repeat from * across. **Rows 3 and 9:** * Sl 1 as if to p, k 2, sl 3 as if to p, k 2, sl 2 as if to p, repeat from * across. **Rows 4 and 8:** * Sl 1, p 2, sl 3, p 2, sl 2, repeat from * across. **Rows 5 and 7:** * Sl 3 as if to p, k 2, repeat from * across. **Row 6:** * P 1, sl 3, p 1, repeat from * across. **Rows 12 and 14:** P. **Row 13:** K.

[69]
Multiple of 4 sts plus 2: **Row 1:** * K 2, k the 2nd st on left-hand needle, k the 1st st and drop both sts from left-hand needle, repeat from * across, and end k 2. **Rows 2 and 4:** P. **Row 3:** K.

43

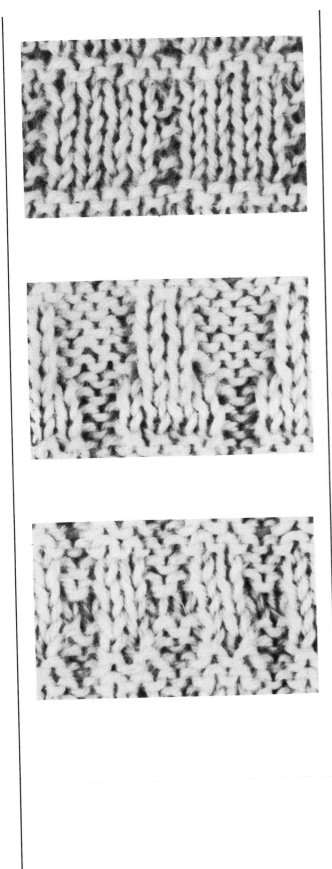

[70]
Multiple of 5 sts: **Rows 1, 3, 5, and 7:** K. **Rows 2, 4, and 6:** * P 4, k 1, repeat from * across. **Row 8:** K.

[71]
Multiple of 6 sts plus 2: **Rows 1 and 3:** * P 2, k 4, repeat from * across and end p 2. **Rows 2, 4, 6, and 8:** K the p sts and p the k sts of previous row. **Rows 5 and 7:** P 3, * k 2, p 4, repeat from * across, and end p 3. **Row 9:** P. **Row 10:** K.

[72]
Multiple of 4 sts: **Rows 1 and 2:** * K 2, p 2, repeat from * across. **Row 3:** K. **Row 4:** P. **Rows 5 and 6:** * K 2, p 2, repeat from * across. **Row 7:** P. **Row 8:** K.

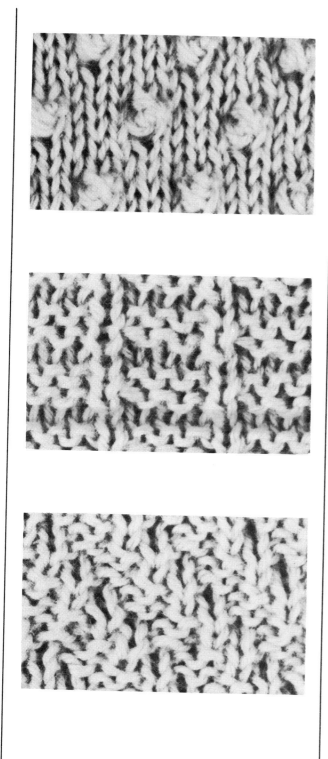

[73]

Multiple of 4 sts plus 3: **Rows 1, 3, and 7:** K. **Rows 2 and 6:** P. **Row 4:** P 3, * (k 1, p 1, k 1, p 1) in next st, p 3, repeat from * across. **Row 5:** * K 3, sl 3 as if to p, k 1, pass separately the 3 sl sts over last k st, repeat from * across, and end k 3. **Row 8:** P 1, * (k 1, p 1, k 1, p 1) in next st, p 3, repeat from * across, and end p 1. **Row 9:** K 1, * sl 3 as if to p, k 1, pass separately the 3 sl sts over last k st, k 3, repeat from * across, and end k 1. Repeat rows 2 through 9 for pattern.

[74]

Multiple of 4 sts plus 3: **Row 1:** P 3, * k 1, p 3, repeat from * across. **Row 2:** K 3, * p 1, k 3, repeat from * across. **Row 3:** K. **Row 4:** P.

[75]

Multiple of 4 sts plus 2: **Rows 1 and 6:** * K 2, p 2, repeat from * across, and end k 2. **Row 2:** * P 2, k 2, repeat from * across, and end p 2. **Rows 3 and 4:** P 1, * k 2, p 2, repeat from * across, and end k 1. **Row 5:** * P 2, k 2, repeat from * across, and end p 2. **Rows 7 and 8:** K 1, * p 2, k 2, repeat from * across, and end p 1.

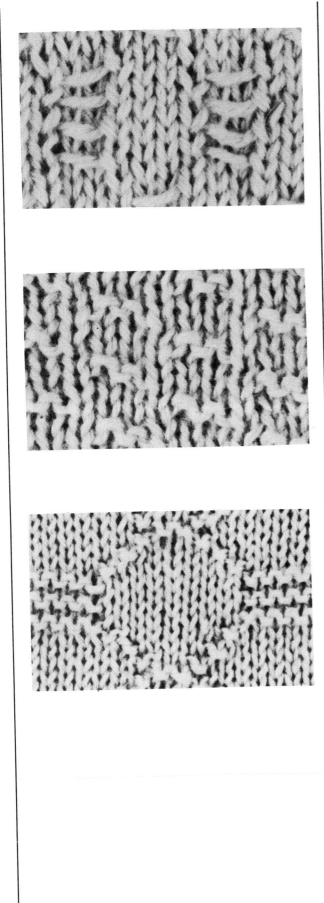

[76]
Multiple of 6 sts plus 4: **Rows 1, 3, 5, and 7:** K 4, * sl 2 as if to p, k 4, repeat from * across. **Rows 2, 4, 6, 8, 10, 12, 14, and 16:** P. **Rows 9, 11, 13, and 15:** K 1, * sl 2 as if to p, k 4, repeat from * across, and end sl 2 as if to p, k 1.

[77]
Multiple of 6 sts plus 2: **Row 1:** K 3, p 2, * k 4, p 2, repeat from * across, and end k 3. **Rows 2 and 4:** P. **Row 3:** P 2, * k 4, p 2, repeat from * across.

[78]
Multiple of 14 sts: **Rows 1, 3, and 5 (right side):** K 4, * p 6, k 8, repeat from * across, and end p 6, k 4. **Rows 2 and 4:** P. **Rows 6 and 12:** P 3, k 1, * p 6, k 1, repeat from * across, and end p 3. **Rows 7 and 11:** K 2, p 1, * k 8, p 1, k 4, p 1, repeat from * across, and end k 8, p 1, k 2. **Rows 8 and 10:** P 1, k 1, * p 10, k 1, p 2, k 1, repeat from * across, and end p 10, k 1, p 1. **Row 9:** P 1, * k 12, p 2, repeat from * across, and end k 12, p 1.

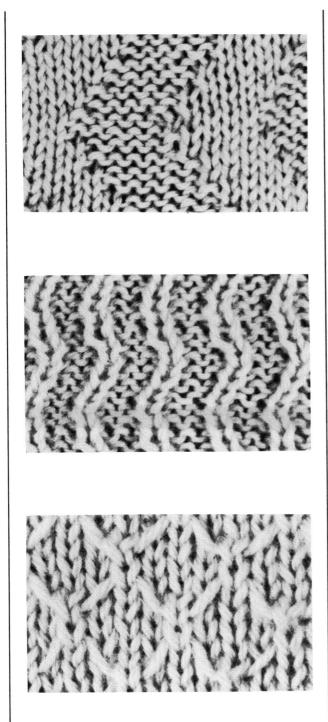

[79]

Multiple of 10 sts plus 2: **Row 1:** K 6, * p 5, k 5, repeat from * across, and end k 1. **Rows 2, 4, 6, 8, 10, 12, 14, 16, 18, and 20:** K the p sts and p the k sts of previous row. **Rows 3 and 19:** K 1, p 1, * k 5, p 5, repeat from * across, and end p 4, k 1. **Rows 5 and 17:** K 1, p 2, * k 5, p 5, repeat from * across, and end p 3, k 1. **Rows 7 and 15:** K 1, p 3, * k 5, p 5, repeat from * across, and end p 2, k 1. **Rows 9 and 13:** K 1, p 4, * k 5, p 5, repeat from * across, and end p 1, k 1. **Row 11:** K 1, * p 5, k 5, repeat from * across, and end k 6.

[80]

Multiple of 4 sts plus 3: **Row 1:** P 3, * k through front lp of 2nd st, p the 1st st and drop both sts from left-hand needle (right twist), p 2, repeat from * across. **Rows 2 and 6:** K 3, * p 1, k 3, repeat from * across. **Row 3:** P 2, * right twist, p 2, repeat from * across, and end p 3. **Row 4:** K 4, * p 1, k 3, repeat from * across, and end k 2. **Row 5:** P 2, * k the 2nd st on left-hand needle, k the 1st st and drop both sts from left-hand needle (left twist), p 2, repeat from * across, and end p 3. **Row 7:** P 3, * left twist, p 2, repeat from * across. **Row 8:** K 2, * p 1, k 3, repeat from * across, and end k 4.

[81]

Multiple of 4 sts plus 1: **Rows 1, 3, 5, and 7 (wrong side):** P. **Row 2:** K 1, * sl 3 as if to p, k 1, repeat from * across. **Row 4:** K 2, * insert needle under strand, into next st, and k as 1 st, k 3, repeat from * across, and end k 2. **Row 6:** K 3, * sl 3 as if to p, k 1, repeat from * across, and end k 3. **Row 8:** K 4, * insert needle under strand, into next st, and k as 1 st, k 3, repeat from * across, and end k 4.

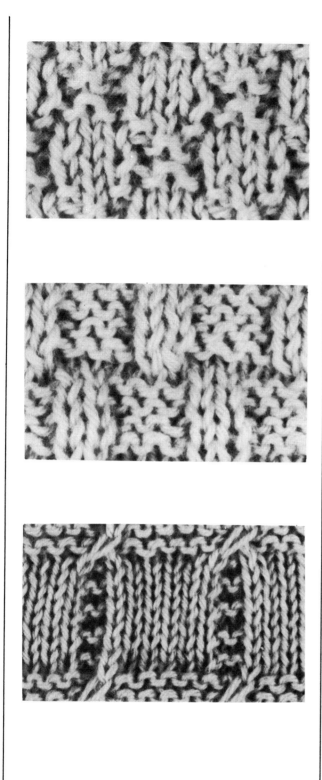

[82]

Multiple of 6 sts plus 3: **Rows 1 and 3:** K 3, * p 3, k 3, repeat from * across. **Rows 2 and 4:** P 3, * k 1, p 1, k 1, p 3, repeat from * across. **Rows 5 and 7:** P 3, * k 3, p 3, repeat from * across. **Rows 6 and 8:** K 1, p 1, k 1, * p 3, k 1, p 1, k 1, repeat from * across.

[83]

Multiple of 6 sts: **Rows 1 and 7:** K. **Rows 2 and 8:** P. **Row 3:** * P 4, k 2, repeat from * across. **Rows 4, 5, 6, 10, 11, and 12:** K the p sts and p the k sts of previous row. **Row 9:** * K 2, p 4, repeat from * across.

[84]

Multiple of 8 sts plus 2: **Rows 1, 3, 5, and 7:** K. **Rows 2, 4, 6, 8, and 14:** * K 2, p 6, repeat from * across, and end k 2. **Row 9:** K 7, * sl 1, k 2, sl 1, k 4, repeat from * across, and end k 7. **Row 10:** K 7, * sl 1 as if to p, k 2, sl 1 as if to p, k 4, repeat from * across, and end k 7. **Row 11:** K 7, * sl 1 as if to p, k 2, sl 1 as if to p, k 4, repeat from * across, and end k 7. **Row 12:** K 7, * sl 1 as if to p, k 2, sl 1 as if to p, k 4, repeat from * across, and end k 7. **Row 13:** K 7, * sl 3 sts on dp needle, hold in back of work, k 1, k 3 from dp needle, k 4, repeat from * across, and end k 7.

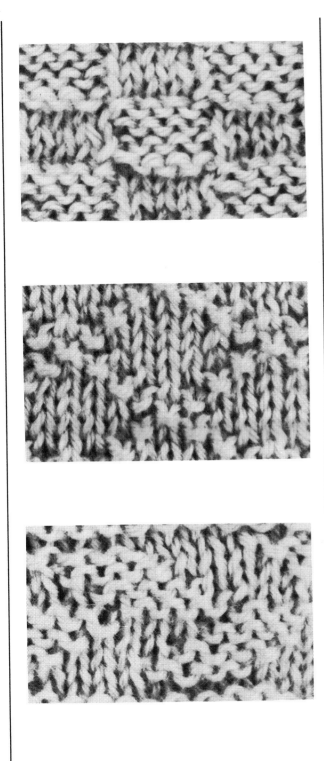

[85]
Multiple of 8 sts: **Rows 1, 2, 3, and 4:** * K 4, p 4, repeat from * across. **Rows 5, 6, 7, and 8:** * P 4, k 4, repeat from * across.

[86]
Multiple of 8 sts plus 1: **Row 1:** K 4, * p 1, k 7, repeat from * across, and end p 1, k 4. **Rows 2 and 8:** P 3, * k 1, p 1, k 1, p 5, repeat from * across, and end p 3. **Rows 3 and 7:** K 2, * p 1, k 3, repeat from * across, and end k 2. **Rows 4 and 6:** * P 1, k 1, p 5, k 1, repeat from * across, and end p 1. **Row 5:** * P 1, k 7, repeat from * across, and end p 1.

[87]
Multiple of 8 sts: **Rows 1, 4, and 14:** P. **Rows 2, 3, and 13:** K. **Row 5:** * K 4, p 4, repeat from * across. **Rows 6 and 9:** K 3, * p 4, k 4, repeat from * across, and end k 1. **Rows 7 and 10:** P 2, * k 4, p 4, repeat from * across, and end p 2. **Rows 8 and 11:** K 1, * p 4, k 4, repeat from * across, and end k 3. **Row 12:** * P 4, k 4, repeat from * across, and end k 4.

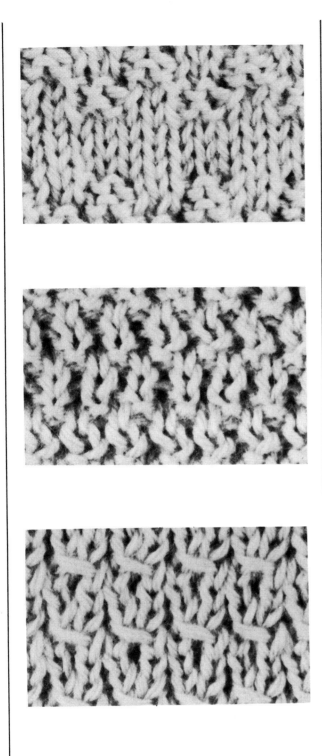

[88]

Multiple of 4 sts: **Rows 1, 3, 9, and 11:** K. **Rows 2, 4, 10, and 12:** P. **Rows 5, 6, 15, and 16:** * K 2, p 2, repeat from * across. **Rows 7, 8, 13, and 14:** * P 2, k 2, repeat from * across.

[89]

Multiple of 2 sts plus 1: **Rows 1, 3, 4, and 6:** K 1, * p 1, k 1, repeat from * across. **Rows 2 and 5:** P 1, * k 1, p 1, repeat from * across.

[90]

Multiple of 3 sts plus 1: **Row 1 (wrong side):** K 1, * p 2, k 1, repeat from * across. **Row 2:** P 1, * k 1, yo, k 1, p 1, repeat from * across. **Row 3:** K 1, * p 3, k 1, repeat from * across. **Row 4:** P 1, * sl 1, k 2, psso 2 sts just worked, p 1, repeat from * across.

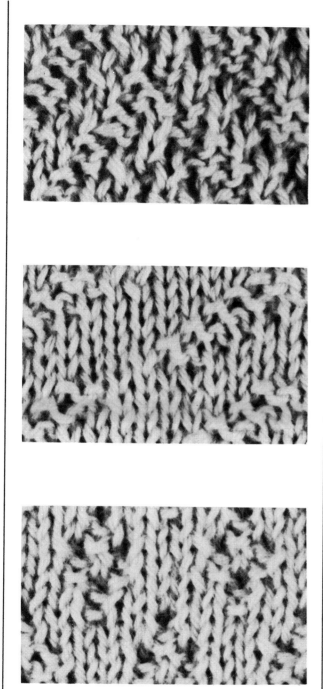

[91]

Multiple of 12 sts: **Row 1:** * P 2, k 2, p 2, k 1, p 2, k 2, p 1, repeat from * across. **Rows 2, 4, 6, and 8:** K the p sts and p the k sts of previous row. **Row 3:** * P 1, k 2, p 2, k 3, p 2, k 2, repeat from * across. **Row 5:** * K 2, p 2, k 2, p 1, k 2, p 2, k 1, repeat from * across. **Row 7:** * K 1, p 2, k 2, p 3, k 2, p 2, repeat from * across.

[92]

Multiple of 8 sts: **Row 1:** * K 6, p 2, repeat from * across. **Row 2:** * P 1, k 2, p 5, repeat from * across. **Row 3:** * K 4, p 2, k 2, repeat from * across. **Row 4:** * P 3, k 2, p 3, repeat from * across. **Row 5:** * K 2, p 2, k 4, repeat from * across. **Row 6:** P.

[93]

Multiple of 6 sts: **Rows 1 and 5:** * K 1, p 1, k 4, repeat from * across. **Rows 2, 4, 6, 8, 10, and 12:** K the p sts and p the k sts of previous row. **Row 3:** * P 1, k 1, p 1, k 3, repeat from * across. **Rows 7 and 11:** * K 4, p 1, k 1, repeat from * across. **Row 9:** * K 3, p 1, k 1, p 1, repeat from * across.

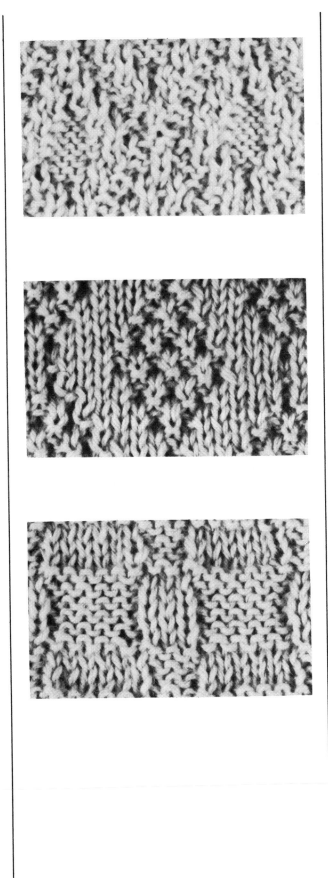

[94]
Multiple of 12 sts: **Row 1:** * K 2, p 5, k 2, p 3, repeat from * across. **Rows 2, 4, 6, 8, 10, 12, 14, 16, 18, and 20:** K the p sts and p the k sts of previous row. **Rows 3 and 19:** * P 1, k 2, p 3, k 2, p 2, k 1, p 1, repeat from * across. **Rows 5 and 17:** * P 2, k 2, p 1, k 2, p 2, k 3, repeat from * across. **Rows 7 and 15:** * K 1, p 2, k 3, p 2, k 2, p 1, k 1, repeat from * across. **Rows 9 and 13:** * K 2, p 2, k 1, p 2, k 2, p 3, repeat from * across. **Row 11:** * P 1, k 2, p 3, k 2, p 4, repeat from * across.

[95]
Multiple of 14 sts: **Row 1:** * (P 1, k 1) 4 times, k 6, repeat from * across. **Rows 2, 4, 6, 8, 10, 12, 14, and 16:** K the p sts and p the k sts of previous row. **Rows 3 and 15:** * (K 1, p 1) 3 times, k 4, p 1, k 3, repeat from * across. **Rows 5 and 13:** * K 2, p 1, k 1, p 1, k 4, p 1, k 1, p 1, k 2, repeat from * across. **Rows 7 and 11:** * K 3, p 1, k 4, (p 1, k 1) 3 times, repeat from * across. **Row 9:** * K 6, (k 1, p 1) 4 times, repeat from * across.

[96]
Multiple of 9 sts plus 6: **Rows 1, 3, and 5:** * P 6, k 3, repeat from * across, and end p 6. **Rows 2, 4, 6, 8, and 10:** K the p sts and p the k sts of previous row. **Rows 7 and 9:** * K 6, p 3, repeat from * across, and end k 6.

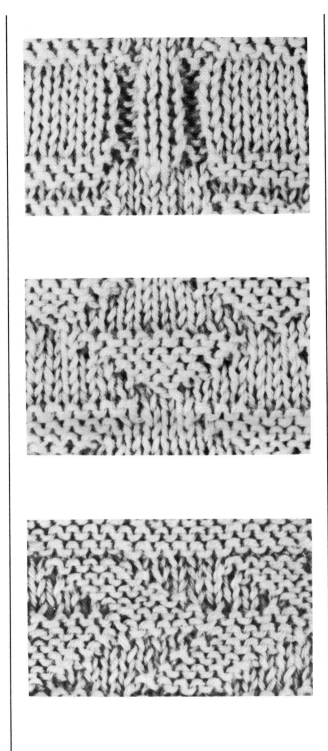

[97]
Multiple of 12 sts: **Rows 1 and 11:** * K 2, p 6, k 4, repeat from * across. **Rows 2, 4, 6, 8, 10, and 12:** K the p sts and p the k sts of previous row. **Rows 3, 5, 7, and 9:** * P 2, k 6, p 2, k 2, repeat from * across. **Row 13:** K. **Row 14:** P.

[98]
Multiple of 12 sts: **Row 1:** * K 6, p 1, k 5, repeat from * across. **Row 2:** * P 4, k 3, p 5, repeat from * across. **Row 3:** * K 4, p 5, k 3, repeat from * across. **Row 4:** * P 2, k 7, p 3, repeat from * across. **Row 5:** * K 2, p 9, k 1, repeat from * across. **Rows 6 and 12:** P. **Row 7:** * P 1, k 11, repeat from * across. **Row 8:** * K 1, p 9, k 2, repeat from * across. **Row 9:** * P 3, k 7, p 2, repeat from * across. **Row 10:** * K 3, p 5, k 4, repeat from * across. **Row 11:** * P 5, k 3, p 4, repeat from * across.

[99]
Multiple of 10 sts: **Rows 1, 3, 4, and 16:** P. **Row 2:** K. **Row 5:** * P 5, k 5, repeat from * across. **Row 6:** * K 1, p 5, k 4, repeat from * across. **Row 7:** * P 3, k 5, p 2, repeat from * across. **Row 8:** * K 3, p 5, k 2, repeat from * across. **Row 9:** * P 1, k 5, p 4, repeat from * across. **Row 10:** K. **Row 11:** * K 1, p 5, k 4, repeat from * across. **Row 12:** * P 3, k 5, p 2, repeat from * across. **Row 13:** * K 3, p 5, k 2, repeat from * across. **Row 14:** * P 1, k 5, p 4, repeat from * across. **Row 15:** * K 5, p 5, repeat from * across.

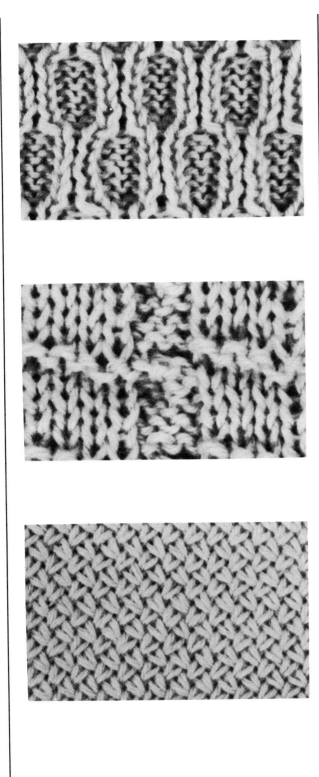

[100]

Multiple of 6 sts: **Rows 1 and 3:** * P 2, k 2, p 2, repeat from * across. **Rows 2, 4, 6, 8, 10, and 12:** K the p sts and p the k sts of previous row. **Row 5:** * Sl 2 on dp needle and hold in back, k 1, p 2 from dp needle, sl 1 on dp needle and hold in front, p 2, k 1 from dp needle, repeat from * across. **Rows 7 and 9:** * K 1, p 4, k 1, repeat from * across. **Row 11:** * Sl 1 on dp needle, hold in front, p 2, k 1 from dp needle, sl 2 on dp needle, hold in back, k 1, p 2 from dp needle, repeat from * across.

[101]

Multiple of 8 sts: **Rows 1, 2, 3, 4, and 6:** * K 4, p 4, repeat from * across. **Row 5:** * P 4, sl 2 on dp needle, hold in front, k 2, k 2 from dp needle, repeat from * across.

[102]

Multiple of 2 sts plus 1: **Row 1:** K 1, * k the 2nd st, k the 1st st and drop both sts from left-hand needle, repeat from * across. **Row 2:** P 1, * p the 2nd st on left-hand needle, p the 1st st and drop both sts from left-hand needle, repeat from * across.

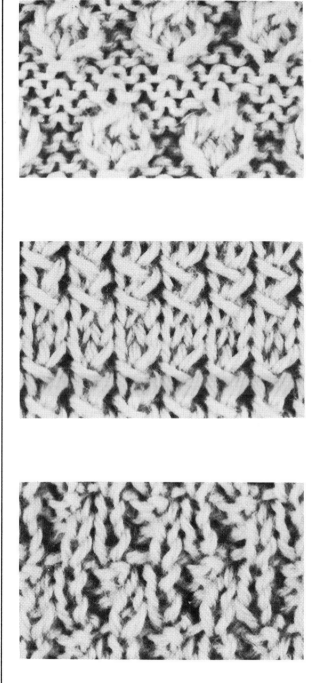

[103]

Multiple of 4 sts: **Row 1:** * P 3, (k 1, yo, k 1) in next st, repeat from * across. **Rows 2 and 3:** * P 3, k 3, repeat from * across. **Row 4:** * P 3 tog, k 3, repeat from * across. **Rows 5 and 11:** P. **Rows 6 and 12:** K. **Row 7:** * P 1, (k 1, yo, k 1) in next st, p 2, repeat from * across. **Row 8:** K 2, * p 3, k 3, repeat from * across, and end p 3, k 1. **Row 9:** P 1, * k 3, p 3, repeat from * across, and end k 3, p 2. **Row 10:** K 2, * p 3 tog, k 3, repeat from * across, and end p 3 tog, k 1.

[104]

Multiple of 2 sts: **Rows 1 and 3:** * Sl 1 as if to p, k 1, yo, psso the k 1 and yo, repeat from * across. **Rows 2, 4, and 6:** P. **Row 5:** K.

[105]

Multiple of 4 sts: **Row 1:** * K the 2nd st on left-hand needle, p the 1st st and drop both sts from left-hand needle (right twist), p the 2nd st on left-hand needle, k the 1st st and drop both sts from left-hand needle (left twist), repeat from * across. **Rows 2, 4, and 7:** * P 1, k 2, p 1, repeat from * across. **Rows 3, 6, and 8:** * K 1, p 2, k 1, repeat from * across. **Row 5:** * Left twist, right twist, repeat from * across.

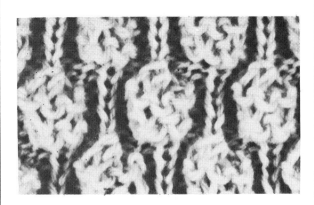

[106]
Multiple of 6 sts plus 2: **Row 1 (right side):** P 2, *(k in front and back of next st) twice, p 2, k 1, p 2, repeat from * across. **Rows 2 and 4:** * K 2, p 1, k 2, (k 1, wrapping yarn around needle twice) 4 times, repeat from * across, and end k 2. **Rows 3 and 5:** P 2, * (k 1, dropping the extra lp) 4 times, p 2, k 1, p 2, repeat from * across. **Row 6:** * K 2, p 1, k 2, p 4 tog, repeat from * across, and end k 2. **Row 7:** P 2, * k 1, p 2, (k in front and back of next st) twice, p 2, repeat from * across. **Rows 8 and 10:** * K 2, (k 1, wrapping yarn around needle twice) 4 times, k 2, p 1, repeat from * across, and end k 2. **Rows 9 and 11:** P 2, * k 1, p 2, (k 1, dropping the extra lp) 4 times, p 2, repeat from * across. **Row 12:** * K 2, p 4 tog, k 2, p 1, repeat from * across, and end k 2.

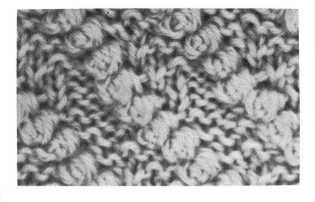

[107]
Multiple of 6 sts: **Row 1:** * K 2, k in front and back of next st 3 times, pass the 2nd, 3rd, 4th, 5th, and 6th sts over 1st st (popcorn made), p 3, repeat from * across, and end p 3. **Rows 2, 4, 6, 8, 10, and 12:** * K 3, p 3, repeat from * across. **Row 3:** * P 1, k 2, popcorn, p 2, repeat from * across. **Row 5:** * P 2, k 2, popcorn, p 1, repeat from * across. **Row 7:** * P 3, k 2, popcorn, repeat from * across. **Row 9:** * Popcorn, p 3, k 2, repeat from * across. **Row 11:** * K 1, popcorn, p 3, k 1, repeat from * across.

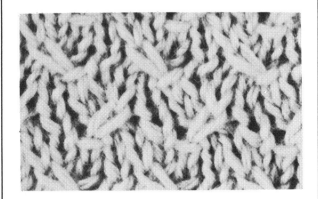

[108]
Multiple of 4 sts plus 1: **Rows 1 and 5:** * K 2, sl 1 as if to p, k 1, repeat from * across, and end k 2. **Rows 2 and 6:** P 1, * p 1, sl 1, p 2, repeat from * across. **Row 3:** * Sl 2 on dp needle, hold in back, k 1, k 2 from dp needle, k 1, repeat from * across, and end k 2. **Rows 4 and 8:** P. **Row 7:** K 1, * k 1, sl 1 on dp needle, hold in front, k 2, k 1 from dp needle, repeat from * across.

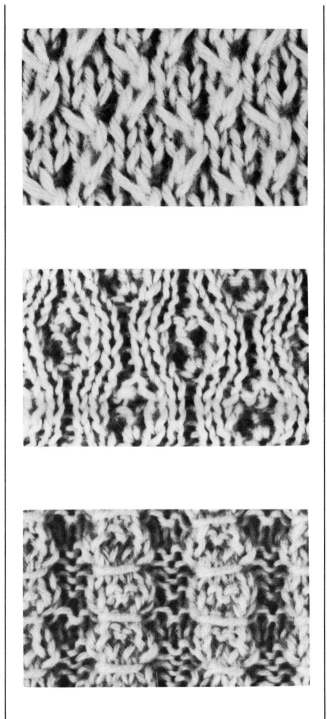

[109]

Multiple of 4 sts: **Row 1:** * K in front of the 2nd st on left-hand needle, k the 1st st and drop both sts from left-hand needle (right twist), k the 2nd st on left-hand needle, k the 1st st and drop both sts from left-hand needle (left twist), repeat from * across. **Row 2:** P. **Row 3:** K. **Row 4:** Sl 1, * p 2, sl 2, repeat from * across, and end p 2, sl 1. **Row 5:** * Left twist, right twist, repeat from * across. **Row 6:** P. **Row 7:** K. **Row 8:** P 1, * sl 2, p 2, repeat from * across, and end sl 2, p 1.

[110]

Multiple of 6 sts plus 2: **Row 1 (wrong side):** P 2, * (k in front and back of next st) twice, p 2, k 1, p 2, repeat from * across. **Rows 2 and 4:** * K 2, p 1, k 2, (k 1, wrapping yarn around needle twice) 4 times, repeat from * across, and end k 2. **Rows 3 and 5:** P 2, * (k 1, dropping the extra lp) 4 times, p 2, k 1, p 2, repeat from * across. **Row 6:** * K 2, p 1, k 2, p 4 tog, repeat from * across, and end k 2. **Row 7:** P 2, * k 1, p 2, (k in front and back of next st) twice, p 2, repeat from * across. **Rows 8 and 10:** * K 2, (k 1, wrapping yarn around needle twice) 4 times, k 2, p 1, repeat from * across, and end k 2. **Rows 9 and 11:** P 2, * k 1, p 2, (k 1, dropping the extra lp) 4 times, p 2, repeat from * across. **Row 12:** * K 2, p 4 tog, k 2, p 1, repeat from * across, and end k 2.

[111]

Multiple of 6 sts plus 4: **Row 1:** K 4, * p 2, k 4, repeat from * across. **Rows 2 and 4:** P 4, * k 2, p 4, repeat from * across. **Rows 3 and 7:** Insert needle between 4th and 5th sts on left-hand needle and draw up a lp, k 4, pass lp over last 4 sts, * p 2, draw up a lp between 4th and 5th sts on left-hand needle, k 4, pass lp over 4 sts, repeat from * across. **Row 5:** K 1, * p 2, k 4, repeat from * across, and end p 2, k 1. **Rows 6 and 8:** P 1, * k 2, p 4, repeat from * across, and end k 2, p 1.

[112]
Multiple of 14 sts: **Rows 1 and 5:** * P 2, k 3, p 4, k 3, p 2, repeat from * across. **Rows 2 and 6:** * K 2, p 3, k 4, p 3, k 2, repeat from * across. **Row 3:** * P 2, k 3, p 4, yo, sl 1 as if to p, k 2 tog, psso, yo, p 2, repeat from * across. **Row 4:** * K 2, p 3, k 4, p 3, k 2, repeat from * across. **Row 7:** * P 2, yo, sl 1 as if to p, k 2.

[113]
Multiple of 6 sts: **Row 1:** * Sl 3 as if to k, sl 3 as if to p, repeat from * across. **Rows 2, 4, 6, 8, 10, and 12:** P. **Row 3:** K 1, * sl 3 as if to p, k 3, repeat from * across, and end k 2. **Row 5:** K 2, * sl 3 as if to p, k 3, repeat from * across, and end k 1. **Row 7:** * K 3, sl 3 as if to p, repeat from * across. **Row 9:** Sl 1 as if to p, * k 3, sl 3 as if to p, repeat from * across, and end sl 2. **Row 11:** Sl 2 as if to p, * k 3, sl 3 as if to p, repeat from * across, and end sl 1.

[114]
Multiple of 8 sts plus 3: **Rows 1, 3, 7, and 9:** * P 3, k 1, repeat from * across, and end p 3. **Rows 2, 4, 6, 8, 10, and 12:** * K 3, p 1, repeat from * across, and end k 3. **Row 5:** * P 3, sl 5, turn, sl 5, turn, sl 5, turn, sl 5, turn, sl 1 as if to k, p 3, k 1 (wrap 5 sts), repeat from * across, and end p 3. **Row 11:** P 3, k 1, p 3, * wrap 5 sts, p 3, repeat from * across, and end p 3, k 1, p 3.

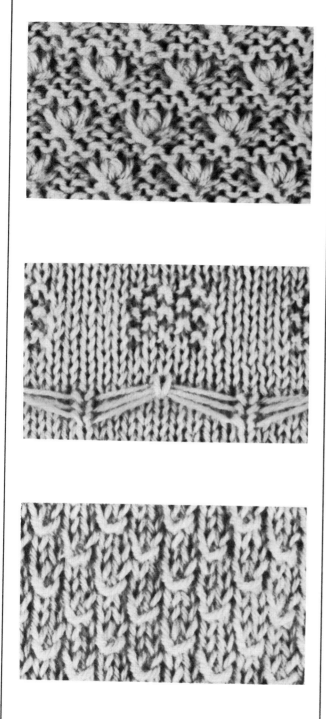

[115]

Multiple of 4 sts plus 2: **Rows 1 and 5:** P. **Rows 2 and 6:** K. **Row 3:** P 2, * insert needle in next 2 sts and p 1, k 1, p 1, k 1 in these 2 sts, p 2, repeat from * across. **Row 4:** K 2, * (p 2 tog) twice, k 2, repeat from * across. **Row 7:** * Insert needle in next 2 sts and p 1, k 1, p 1, k 1 in these 2 sts, p 2, repeat from * across, and end p 1, k 1, p 1, k 1 in last 2 sts. **Row 8:** * (P 2 tog) twice, k 2, repeat from * across, and end (p 2 tog) twice.

[116]

Multiple of 10 sts plus 5: **Rows 1, 3, and 5:** * K 5, p 1, k 1, p 1, k 1, p 1, repeat from * across, and end k 5. **Rows 2, 4, and 6:** * P 6, k 1, p 1, k 1, p 1, repeat from * across, and end p 5. **Rows 7 and 17:** K. **Rows 8, 10, 12, 14, 16, and 18:** P. **Rows 9, 11, and 13:** K 3, * sl 9 as if to p, k 1, repeat from * across, and end k 3. **Row 15:** K 7, * go under 3 strands and k off with next st, k 9, repeat from * across, and end k 7.

[117]

Multiple of 4 sts: **Rows 1 and 3:** K. **Row 2:** * Yo, p 2, pass yo over last 2 sts, p 2, repeat from * across. **Row 4:** * P 2, yo, p 2, pass yo over last 2 sts, repeat from * across.

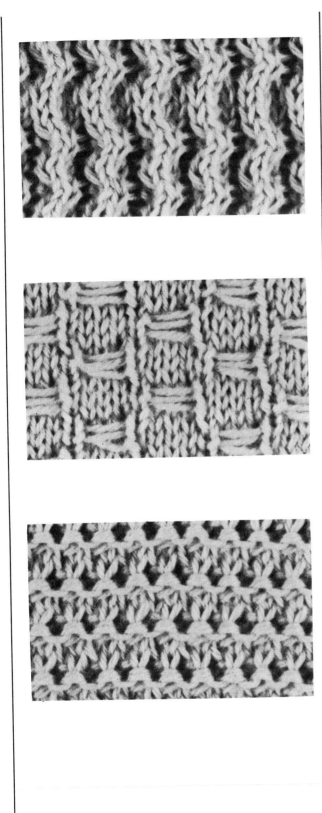

[118]
Multiple of 4 sts: **Row 1:** K. **Rows 2, 4, 6, 8, 10, 12, and 14:** P. **Rows 3, 7, and 11:** K 2, * sl 2 on dp needle, hold in back, k 2, k 2 from dp needle, repeat from * across, and end k 2. **Rows 5, 9, and 13:** K 2, * sl 2 on dp needle, hold in front, k 2, k 2 from dp needle, repeat from * across, and end k 2.

[119]
Multiple of 8 sts plus 1: **Rows 1 and 3:** * K 5, sl 3 as if to p, repeat from * across, and end k 1. **Row 2:** P 1, * sl 3 as if to k, p 5, repeat from * across. **Rows 4 and 8:** P. **Rows 5 and 7:** K 1, * sl 3 as if to p, k 5, repeat from * across. **Row 6:** * P 5, sl 3 as if to k, repeat from * across, and end p 1.

[120]
Multiple of 2 sts: **Row 1:** K. **Row 2:** * K 2 tog, repeat from * across. **Row 3:** * K into front and back of next st, repeat from * across. **Row 4:** P.

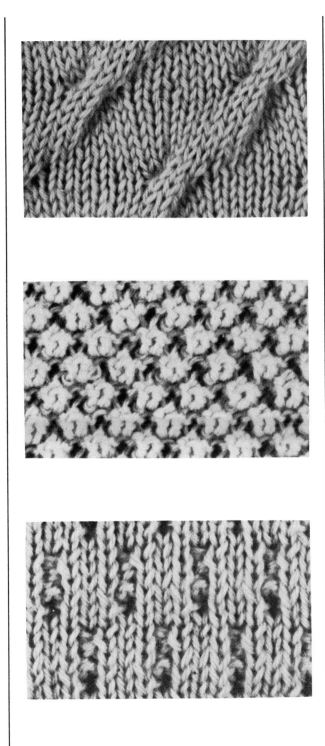

[121]
Multiple of 12 sts plus 7: **Row 1:** K 7, * sl 3 on dp needle, hold in back, k 3, k 3 from dp needle (back twist), k 6, repeat from * across. **Rows 2, 4, 6, 8, 10, 12, 14, and 16:** P. **Rows 3, 5, 7, 11, 13, and 15:** K. **Row 9:** K 1, * back twist, k 6, repeat from * across, and end back twist.

[122]
Multiple of 4 sts: **Rows 1 and 3 (right side):** P. **Row 2:** * P 3 tog, (k 1, p 1, k 1) in next st, repeat from * across. **Row 4:** * (K 1, p 1, k 1) in next st, p 3 tog, repeat from * across.

[123]
Multiple of 4 sts: **Row 1 (wrong side):** * P 3, (k 1, yo, k 1) in next st, repeat from * across. **Rows 2 and 3:** * P 3, k 3, repeat from * across. **Row 4:** * P 3 tog, k 3, repeat from * across. **Rows 5 and 11:** P. **Rows 6 and 12:** K. **Row 7:** * P 1, (k 1, yo, k 1) in next st, p 2, repeat from * across. **Row 8:** K 2, * p 3, k 3, repeat from * across, and end p 3, k 1. **Row 9:** P 1, * k 3, p 3, repeat from * across, and end k 3, p 2. **Row 10:** K 2, * p 3 tog, k 3, repeat from * across, and end p 3 tog, k 1.

[124]
Multiple of 4 sts: **Row 1 (wrong side):** * K the 2nd st on left-hand needle, p the 1st st and drop both sts from left-hand needle (right twist), p the 2nd st on left-hand needle, k the 1st st and drop both sts from left-hand needle (left twist), repeat from * across. **Rows 2, 4, and 7:** * P 1, k 2, p 1, repeat from * across. **Rows 3, 6, and 8:** * K 1, p 2, k 1, repeat from * across. **Row 5:** * Left twist, right twist, repeat from * across.

[125]
Multiple of 2 sts plus 1: **Rows 1, 3, 4, and 6:** K 1, * p 1, k 1, repeat from * across. **Rows 2 and 5:** P 1, * k 1, p 1, repeat from * across.

[126]
Multiple of 10 sts: **Rows 1 and 3:** * Yo, k 3, sl 1, k 2 tog, psso, k 3, yo, k 1, repeat from * across. **Row 2:** P. **Row 4:** K.

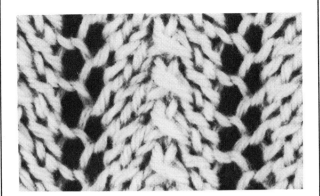

[127]
Multiple of 7 sts: **Row 1:** * K 2, sl 1, k 2 tog, psso, k 2, yo, repeat from * across. **Row 2:** * P 6, yo, repeat from * across, and end p 5, inc 1 st in last st.

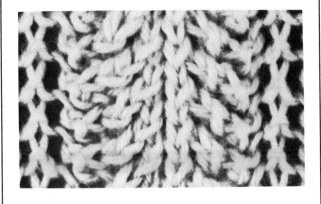

[128]
Multiple of 11 sts: **Row 1:** K. **Row 2:** * (P 2 tog) twice, (yo, k 1) 3 times, yo, (p 2 tog) twice, repeat from * across.

[129]
Multiple of 5 sts: **Rows 1 and 3:** * K 3, p 2, repeat from * across. **Rows 2, 4, and 6:** * K 2, p 3, repeat from * across. **Row 5:** * Yo, sl 1, k 2 tog, psso, yo, p 2, repeat from * across.

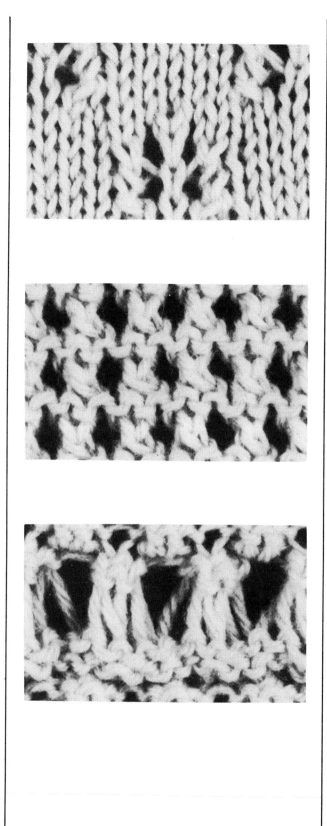

[130]
Multiple of 10 sts: **Rows 1 and 3:** * K 2 tog, yo, k 1, yo, sl 1, k 1, psso, k 5, repeat from * across. **Rows 2 and 4:** * P 7, sl 1, p 2, repeat from * across. **Rows 5 and 11:** K. **Rows 6 and 12:** P. **Rows 7 and 9:** * K 5, k 2 tog, yo, k 1, yo, sl 1, k 1, psso, repeat from * across. **Rows 8 and 10:** * P 2, sl 1, p 7, repeat from * across.

[131]
Multiple of 2 sts: **Rows 1, 2, and 3:** P. **Row 4 (right side):** * Yo, sl 1, k 1, psso, repeat from * across.

[132]
Multiple of 4 sts plus 2: **Row 1 (wrong side):** K 1, * p 3 tog, (k 1, p 1, k 1) in next st, repeat from * across, and end k 1. **Rows 2 and 4:** P. **Row 3:** K 1, * (k 1, p 1, k 1) in next st, p 3 tog, repeat from * across, and end k 1. **Row 5:** K, wrapping yarn 3 times around needle for each st. **Row 6:** P, letting extra lps drop off needle.

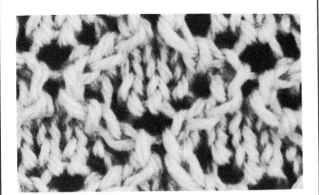

[133]
Multiple of 7 sts: **Row 1:** * K 2, k 2 tog, yo, k 3, repeat from * across. **Row 2:** * P 1, p 2 tog, yo, p 1, yo, p 2 tog, p 1, repeat from * across. **Row 3:** * K 2 tog, yo, k 3, yo, sl 1, k 1, psso, repeat from * across. **Rows 4 and 8:** P. **Row 5:** * Yo, sl 1, k 1, psso, k 5, repeat from * across. **Row 6:** * Yo, p 2 tog, p 2, p 2 tog, yo, p 1, repeat from * across. **Row 7:** * K 2, yo, sl 1, k 1, psso, k 2 tog, yo, k 1, repeat from * across.

[134]
Multiple of 4 sts: **Row 1:** K. **Row 2:** * P 4, yo, repeat from * across, and end p 4. **Row 3:** Dropping yo's of previous row, * sl 1, k 3, psso, repeat from * across. **Row 4:** * Yo, p 3, repeat from * across.

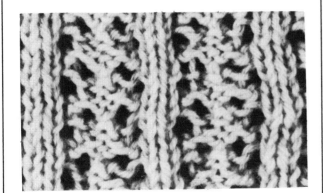

[135]
Multiple of 7 sts plus 2: **Row 1 (wrong side):** P 2, * yo, sl 1, k 1, psso, k 1, sl 1, k 1, psso, yo, p 2, repeat from * across. **Rows 2 and 4:** * K 2, p 5, repeat from * across, and end k 2. **Row 3:** P 2, * k 1, yo, sl 1, k 2 tog, psso, yo, k 1, p 2, repeat from * across.

[136]
Multiple of 3 sts plus 2: **Row 1:** * P 2, yo, k 1, yo, repeat from * across, and end p 2. **Row 2:** K 2, * p 3, k 2, repeat from * across. **Row 3:** * P 2, k 3, repeat from * across, and end p 2. **Row 4:** K 2, * p 3 tog, k 2, repeat from * across.

[137]
Multiple of 6 sts: **Row 1:** * P 2, yo, sl 1, k 1, psso, k 2 tog, yo, repeat from * across, and end k 2. **Rows 2 and 4:** * P 4, k 2, repeat from * across. **Row 3:** * P 2, k 4, repeat from * across.

[138]
Multiple of 3 sts: **Row 1:** * K 1, yo, k 2 tog, repeat from * across. Repeat this row for pattern.

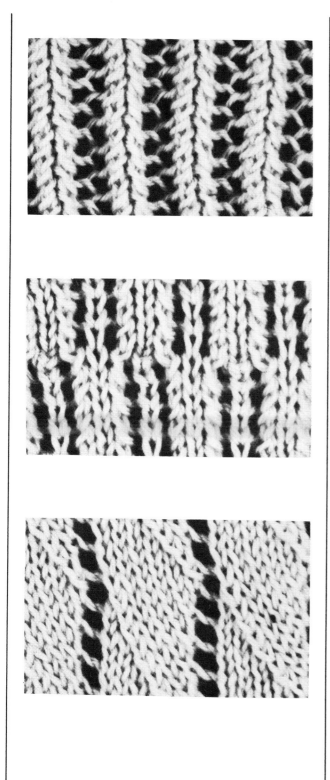

[139]
Multiple of 4 sts: **Row 1:** * K 2, yo, sl 1, k 1; psso, repeat from * across. **Row 2:** * P 2, yo, p 2 tog, repeat from * across.

[140]
Multiple of 6 sts plus 1: **Rows 1, 3, 5, and 7:** * K 1, k 2 tog, yo, k 1, yo, sl 1, k 1, psso, repeat from * across, and end k 1. **Rows 2, 4, 6, 8, 10, 12, 14, and 16:** P. **Rows 9, 11, 13, and 15:** * K 1, yo, sl 1, k 1, psso, k 1, k 2 tog, yo, repeat from * across, and end k 1.

[141]
Multiple of 7 sts plus 4: **Row 1:** K 2, * yo, sl 1, k 1, psso, k 5, repeat from * across, and end yo, k 2 tog. **Rows 2, 4, 6, 8, 10, and 12:** P. **Row 3:** K 2, * yo, k 1, sl 1, k 1, psso, k 4, repeat from * across, and end yo, k 2 tog. **Row 5:** K 2, * yo, k 2, sl 1, k 1, psso, k 3, repeat from * across, and end yo, k 2 tog. **Row 7:** K 2, * yo, k 3, sl 1, k 1, psso, k 2, repeat from * across, and end yo, k 2 tog. **Row 9:** K 2, * yo, k 4, sl 1, k 1, psso, k 1, repeat from * across, and end yo, k 2 tog. **Row 11:** K 2, * yo, k 5, sl 1, k 1, psso, repeat from * across, and end yo, k 2 tog.

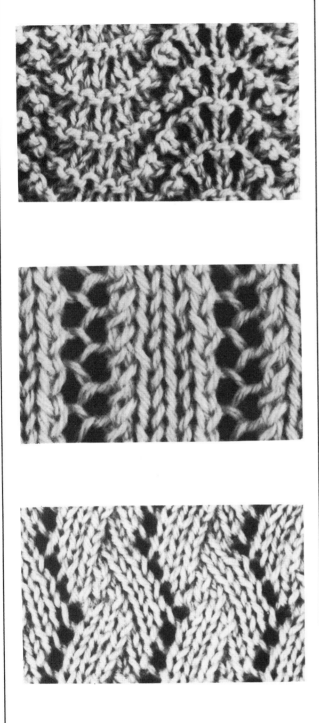

[142]
Multiple of 18 sts: **Rows 1 and 4:** K. **Row 2:** P. **Row 3:** (k 2 tog) 3 times, * (yo, k 1) 6 times, (k 2 tog) 6 times, repeat from * across, and end (k 2 tog) 3 times.

[143]
Multiple of 6 sts: **Row 1:** * K 4, k 2 tog, yo, repeat from * across, and end k 6. **Row 2:** * P 4, p 2 tog, yo, repeat from * across, and end p 6.

[144]
Multiple of 6 sts: **Rows 1, 3, and 5:** * K 2 tog, k 2, yo, k 2, repeat from * across. **Rows 2, 4, 6, 8, 10, and 12:** P. **Rows 7, 9, and 11:** K 1, * k 2, yo, k 2, k 2 tog, repeat from * across, and end yo, k 2 tog, k 1.

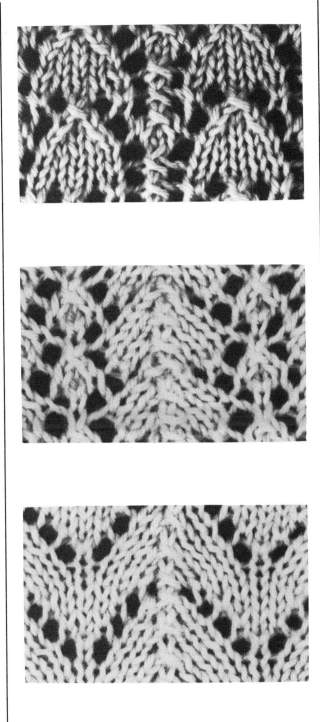

[145]
Multiple of 8 sts plus 3: **Rows 1 and 3:** * Yo, sl 1 as if to p, k 2 tog, psso, yo, k 5, repeat from * across, and end yo, sl 1 as if to p, k 2 tog, psso, yo. **Rows 2, 4, 6, and 8:** P. **Row 5:** * K 3, yo, sl 1, k 1, psso, k 1, k 2 tog, yo, repeat from * across, and end k 3. **Row 7:** * Yo, sl 1, k 2 tog, psso, yo, k 1, repeat from * across, and end yo, sl 1, k 1, psso, k 1.

[146]
Multiple of 10 sts plus 1: **Row 1:** K 1, yo, * k 3, sl 1, k 2 tog, psso, k 3, yo, k 1, yo, repeat from * across, and end yo, k 1. **Rows 2, 4, and 6:** P. **Row 3:** K 2, * yo, k 2, sl 1, k 2 tog, psso, k 2, yo, k 3, repeat from * across, and end yo, k 2. **Row 5:** k 2 tog, yo, * k 1, yo, k 1, sl 1, k 2 tog, psso, k 1, yo, k 1, yo, sl 1, k 2 tog, psso, yo, repeat from * across, and end yo, k 2 tog.

[147]
Multiple of 10 sts: **Row 1:** * Yo, k 3, sl 1, k 2 tog, psso, k 3, yo, k 1, repeat from * across. **Rows 2, 4, 6, and 8:** P. **Row 3:** * K 1, yo, k 2, sl 1, k 2 tog, psso, k 2, yo, k 2, repeat from * across. **Row 5:** * K 2, yo, k 1, sl 1, k 2 tog, psso, k 1, yo, k 3, repeat from * across. **Row 7:** * K 3, yo, sl 1, k 2 tog, psso, yo, k 4, repeat from * across.

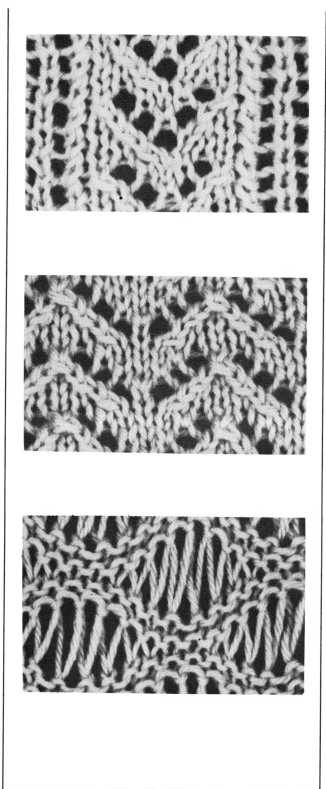

[148]
Multiple of 12 sts: **Row 1:** * K 3, yo, sl 1, k 1, psso, k 2, k 2 tog, yo, k 1, yo, sl 1, k 1, psso, repeat from * across. **Rows 2, 4, and 6:** P. **Row 3:** * K 1, k 2 tog, yo, k 1, yo, sl 1, k 1, psso, repeat from * across. **Row 5:** * K 2 tog, yo, k 3, yo, sl 1, k 1, psso, k 2 tog, yo, k 1, yo, sl 1, k 1, psso, repeat from * across.

[149]
Multiple of 8 sts plus 1: **Row 1:** * K 1, yo, sl 1, k 1, psso, k 3, k 2 tog, yo, repeat from * across, and end k 1. **Rows 2, 4, and 6:** P. **Row 3:** * K 2, yo, sl 1, k 1, psso, k 1, k 2 tog, yo, k 1, repeat from * across, and end k 2. **Row 5:** * K 3, yo, sl 1, k 2 tog, psso, yo, k 2, repeat from * across, and end k 3.

[150]
Multiple of 10 sts plus 2: **Row 1:** K 2, * k 1, 2 yo, k 1, 3 yo, k 1, 4 yo, k 1, 3 yo, k 1, 2 yo, k 5, repeat from * across. **Rows 2 and 6:** K, dropping all yo's of previous row. **Rows 3, 4, 7, and 8:** K. **Row 5:** K 2, * k 6, 2 yo, k 1, 3 yo, k 1, 4 yo, k 1, 3 yo, k 1, 2 yo, repeat from * across, and end 3 yo, k 1.

[151]

Multiple of 5 sts plus 2: **Rows 1 and 3 (wrong side):** * K 2, p 3, repeat from * across, and end k 2. **Row 2:** * P 2, k 3, repeat from * across, and end p 2. **Row 4:** * P 2, yo, sl 1, k 2 tog, psso, yo, repeat from * across, and end p 2.

[152]

Multiple of 19 sts: **Row 1:** * K the 2nd st on left-hand needle, k the 1st st and drop both sts from left-hand needle (front cross), k 2, k 2 tog, yo, k 3, yo, sl 1, k 1, psso, k 2, yo, sl 1, k 1, psso, k 2, front cross, repeat from * across. **Rows 2, 4, 6, 8, 10, 12, 14, 16, and 18:** P the 2nd st on left-hand needle, P the 1st st and drop both sts from left-hand needle (back cross), p to the last 2 sts, back cross. **Row 3:** * Front cross, k 1, k 2 tog, yo, k 2, k 2 tog, yo, k 1, yo, sl 1, k 1, psso, k 2, yo, sl 1, k 1, psso, k 1, front cross, repeat from * across. **Row 5:** * Front cross, k 2 tog, yo, k 2, k 2 tog, yo, k 3, yo, sl 1, k 1, psso, k 2, yo, sl 1, k 1, psso, front cross, repeat from * across. **Row 7:** * Front cross, k 1, yo, sl 1, k 1, psso, k 2, yo, sl 1, k 1, psso, yo, sl 1, k 2 tog, psso, yo, k 2, k 2 tog, yo, k 1, front cross, repeat from * across. **Row 9:** * Front cross, k 2, yo, sl 1, k 1, psso, k 2, yo, sl 1, k 2 tog, psso, yo, k 2, k 2 tog, yo, k 2, front cross, repeat from * across. **Row 11:** * Front cross, k 3, yo, sl 1, k 1, psso, k 2, yo, sl 1, k 1, psso, k 1, k 2 tog, yo, k 3, front cross, repeat from * across. **Row 13:** * Front cross, k 4, yo, sl 1, k 1, psso, k 2, yo, sl 1, k 2 tog, psso, yo, k 4, front cross, repeat from * across. **Row 15:** * Front cross, k 5, yo, sl 1, k 1, psso, k 2, yo, sl 1, k 1, psso, k 4, front cross, repeat from * across. **Row 17:** * Front cross, k 3, k 2 tog, yo, k 1, yo, sl 1, k 1, psso, k 2, yo, sl 1, k 1, psso, k 3, front cross, repeat from * across.

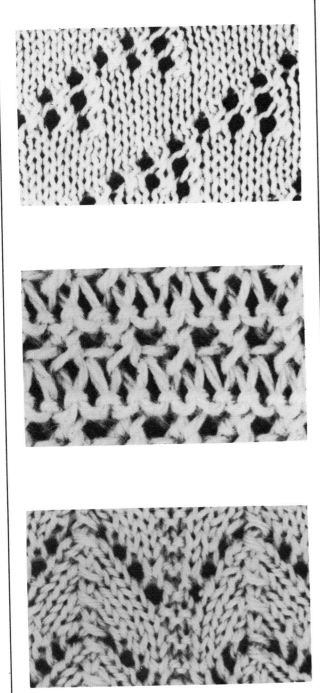

[153]
Multiple of 12 sts plus 6: **Row 1:** K 6, * (k 2 tog, yo) 3 times, k 6, repeat from * across. **Rows 2, 4, 6, 8, 10, and 12:** P. **Row 3:** K 6, * (k 2 tog, yo) twice, k 8, repeat from * across. **Row 5:** K 6, * k 2 tog, yo, k 10, repeat from * across. **Row 7:** * (k 2 tog, yo) 3 times, k 6, repeat from * across, and end (k 2 tog, yo) twice, k 2. **Row 9:** * (k 2 tog, yo) twice, k 8, repeat from * across, and end (k 2 tog, yo) twice, k 2. **Row 11:** * K 2 tog, yo, k 10, repeat from * across, and end k 2 tog, yo, k 4.

[154]
Multiple of 2 sts: **Row 1 (wrong side):** * K 2 tog and leave sts on left-hand needle, p the same 2 sts tog, drop sts from left-hand needle, repeat from * across. **Row 2:** K. **Row 3:** K 1, * yo, k 1, repeat from * across. **Row 4:** K, dropping each yo from left-hand needle.

[155]
Multiple of 11 sts plus 2: **Rows 1, 3, 5, and 7 (wrong side):** P. **Row 2:** * P 2, yo, k 3, sl 1, k 2 tog, psso, k 3, yo, repeat from * across, and end p 2. **Row 4:** * P 2, k 1, yo, k 2, sl 1, k 2 tog, psso, k 2, yo, k 1, repeat from * across, and end p 2. **Row 6:** * P 2, k 2, yo, k 1, sl 1, k 2 tog, psso, k 1, yo, k 2, repeat from * across, and end p 2. **Row 8:** * P 2, k 3, yo, sl 1, k 2 tog, psso, yo, k 3, repeat from * across, and end p 2.

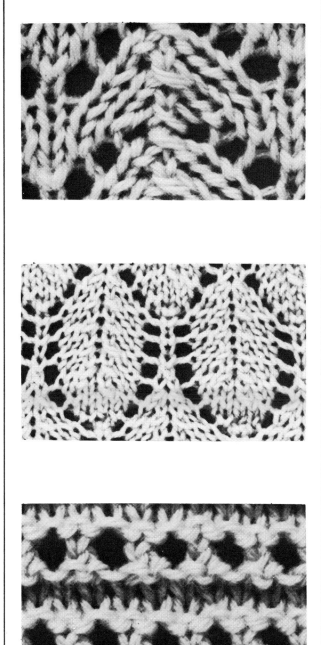

[156]
Multiple of 8 sts plus 1: **Row 1:** * K 1, yo, k 2, sl 1, k 2 tog, psso, k 2, yo, repeat from * across, and end k 1. **Rows 2, 4, and 6:** P. **Row 3:** * K 2, yo, k 1, sl 1, k 2 tog, psso, k 1, yo, k 1, repeat from * across, and end k 1. **Row 5:** * K 3, yo, sl 1, k 2 tog, psso, yo, k 2, repeat from * across, and end k 1.

[157]
Multiple of 9 sts plus 1: **Row 1:** K 1, * yo, k 2, sl 1, k 1, psso, k 3, yo, sl 1, k 1, psso, repeat from * across. **Rows 2, 4, 6, 8, 10, 12, 14, 16, 18, 20, 22, and 24:** P. **Rows 3, 5, and 7:** K 1, * yo, k 2, sl 1, k 1, psso, k 2 tog, k 2, yo, k 1, repeat from * across. **Row 9:** K 1, * k 1, yo, k 1, sl 1, k 1, psso, k 2 tog, k 1, yo, k 2, repeat from * across. **Row 11:** K 1, * k 2, yo, sl 1, k 1, psso, k 2 tog, yo, k 3, repeat from * across. **Row 13:** K 2 tog, * k 2, yo, sl 1, k 1, psso, yo, k 2, sl 1, k 1, psso, k 1, repeat from * across, and end k 2, yo, sl 1, k 1, psso, yo, k 4. **Rows 15, 17, and 19:** K 2 tog, * k 2, yo, k 1, yo, k 2, sl 1, k 1, psso, k 2 tog, repeat from * across, and end k 1. **Row 21:** K 2 tog, * k 1, yo, k 3, yo, k 1, sl 1, k 1, psso, k 2 tog, repeat from * across, and end k 1. **Row 23:** K 2 tog, * yo, k 5, yo, sl 1, k 1, psso, k 2 tog, repeat from * across, and end k 1.

[158]
Multiple of 2 sts: **Rows 1, 3, 4, and 6:** K. **Row 2:** P. **Row 5:** K 1, * yo, k 2 tog, repeat from * across, and end k 1.

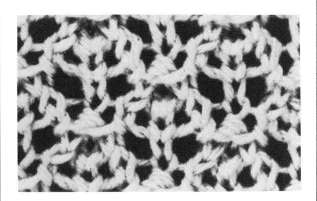

[159]
Multiple of 6 sts plus 1: **Row 1:** K 1, * yo, k 2 tog, k 1, k 2 tog, yo, k 1, repeat from * across. **Rows 2, 4, 6, and 8:** P. **Row 3:** K 1, * yo, k 1, p 3 tog, k 1, yo, k 1, repeat from * across. **Row 5:** K 1, * k 2 tog, yo, k 1, yo, k 2, tog k 1, repeat from * across. **Row 7:** P 2 tog, * (k 1, yo) twice, k 1, p 3 tog, repeat from * across, and end p 2 tog.

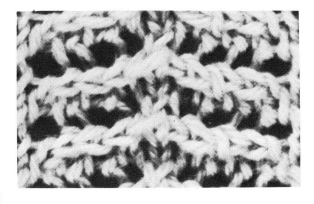

[160]
Multiple of 10 sts plus 3: **Row 1:** K 2, * yo, sl 1, k 1, psso, k 5, k 2 tog, yo, k 1, repeat from * across, and end k 2. **Row 2:** P 3, * yo, p 2 tog, p 3, p 2 tog, yo, p 3, repeat from * across. **Row 3:** K 4, * yo, sl 1, k 1, psso, k 1, k 2 tog, yo, k 5, repeat from * across, and end k 4. **Row 4:** P 5, * yo, p 3 tog, yo, p 7, repeat from * across, and end p 5.

[161]
Multiple of 6 sts plus 1: **Row 1:** * K 1, yo, sl 1, k 1, psso, k 1, k 2 tog, yo, repeat from * across, and end k 1. **Rows 2, 4, 6, and 8:** P. **Row 3:** K 2, * yo, sl 1, k 2 tog, psso, yo, k 3, repeat from * across, and end k 2. **Row 5:** K 1, k 2 tog, * yo, k 1, yo, sl 1, k 1, psso, k 1, k 2 tog, repeat from * across, and end yo, k 1, yo, sl 1, k 1, psso, k 1. **Row 7:** K 2 tog, * yo, k 3, yo, sl 1, k 2 tog, psso, repeat from * across, and end yo, k 3, yo, sl 1, k 1, psso.

[162]
Multiple of 2 sts: **Rows 1, 3, 5, and 7:** * Yo, k 2 tog, repeat from * across. **Rows 2, 4, and 6:** * Yo, p 2 tog, repeat from * across. **Rows 8, 9, and 10:** K.

[163]
Multiple of 4 sts: **Row 1:** * K 3, p 1, repeat from * across. **Rows 2 and 4:** * K 1, p 3, repeat from * across. **Row 3:** * Yo, sl 1 as if to p, k 2 tog, psso, yo, p 1, repeat from * across.

[164]
Multiple of 10 sts: **Rows 1 and 9:** * Yo, sl 1, k 1, psso, k 1, k 2 tog, yo twice, sl 1, k 1, psso, k 1, k 2 tog, yo, repeat from * across. **Rows 2, 4, 6, 8, 10, 12, 14, and 16:** P. **Row 3:** * K 2 tog, yo, k 6, yo, sl 1, k 1, psso, repeat from * across. **Row 5:** * K 1, k 2 tog, yo, k 4, yo, sl 1, k 1, psso, k 1, repeat from * across. **Row 7:** * K 2, k 2 tog, yo, k 2, yo, sl 1, k 1, psso, k 2, repeat from * across. **Row 11:** * K 3, yo, sl 1, k 1, psso, k 2 tog, yo, k 3, repeat from * across. **Row 13:** * K 2, yo, sl 1, k 1, psso, k 2, k 2 tog, yo, k 2, repeat from * across. **Row 15:** * K 1, yo, sl 1, k 1, psso, k 4, k 2 tog, yo, k 1, repeat from * across.

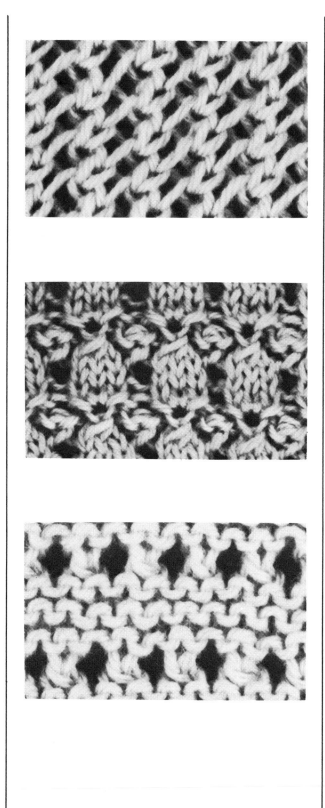

[165]
Multiple of 2 sts: **Row 1:** K 1, * yo, k 2 tog, repeat from * across, and end k 1. Repeat this row for pattern.

[166]
Multiple of 5 sts plus 3: **Row 1:** K 3, * p 2, k 3, repeat from * across. **Row 2:** * P 3, k 1, yo, k 1, repeat from * across, and end p 3. **Row 3:** K 3 * p 1, k 1, p 1, k 3, repeat from * across. **Row 4:** * P 3 tog, (k 1, yo) twice, k 1, repeat from * across, and end p 3 tog. **Row 5:** (K 1, yo, k 1) in next st, * p 1, p 3 tog, p 1, (k 1, yo, k 1) in next st, repeat from * across. **Row 6:** * P 3, sl 1 as if to k, k 1 leaving yarn on left-hand needle, psso, k the yarn on left-hand needle and next st tog, repeat from * across, and end p 3.

[167]
Multiple of 2 sts: **Rows 1, 2, 3, 4, 5, 6, and 7:** P. **Row 8 (right side):** * Yo, sl 1, k 1, psso, repeat from * across.

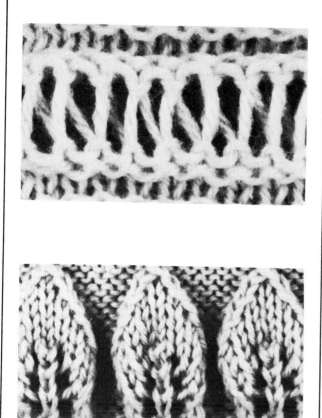

[168]

Multiple of any number of sts: **Row 1:** P, wrapping yarn around needle twice for each st. **Row 2:** K, dropping all extra lps off needle to form long st. **Rows 3, 4, and 6:** P. **Rows 5, 7, and 8:** K.

[169]

Multiple of 7 sts plus 6: **Row 1:** P 6, * yo, k 1, yo, p 6, repeat from * across. **Row 2:** * K 6, p 3, repeat from * across, and end k 6. **Row 3:** P 6, * k 1, yo, k 1, yo, k 1, p 6, repeat from * across. **Row 4:** * K 6, p 5, repeat from * across, and end k 6. **Row 5:** P 6, * k 2, yo, k 1, yo, k 2, p 6, repeat from * across. **Row 6:** * K 6, p 7, repeat from * across, and end k 6. **Row 7:** P 6, * k 3, yo, k 1, yo, k 3, p 6, repeat from * across. **Row 8:** * K 6, p 9, repeat from * across, and end k 6. **Row 9:** P 6, * sl 1, k 1, psso, k 5, k 2 tog, p 6, repeat from * across. **Row 10:** * K 6, p 7, repeat from * across, and end k 6. **Row 11:** P 6, * sl 1, k 1, psso, k 3, k 2 tog, p 6, repeat from * across. **Row 12:** * K 6, p 5, repeat from * across, and end k 6. **Row 13:** P 6, * sl 1, k 1, psso, k 1, k 2 tog, p 6, repeat from * across. **Row 14:** * K 6, p 3, repeat from * across, and end k 6. **Row 15:** P 6, * sl 1, k 2 tog, psso, p 6, repeat from * across. **Rows 16, 18, and 20:** K. **Rows 17 and 19:** P.

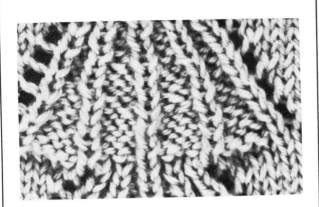

[170]
Multiple of 23 sts: **Row 1:** * K 2, (p 4, k 1) 3 times, p 4, k 2, repeat from * across. **Rows 2, 4, 6, 8, 10, 12, and 14:** K the p sts, and p the k sts and yo's of previous row when they occur. **Row 3:** * K 1, yo, k 1, p 2, p 2 tog, (k 1, p 4) twice, k 1, p 2 tog, p 2, k 1, yo, k 1, repeat from * across. **Row 5:** * K 2, yo, k 1, p 3, k 1, p 2, p 2 tog, k 1, p 2 tog, p 2, k 1, p 3, k 1, yo, k 2, repeat from * across. **Row 7:** * K 3, yo, k 1, p 1, p 2 tog, (k 1, p 3) twice, k 1, p 2 tog, p 1, k 1, yo, k 3, repeat from * across. **Row 9:** * K 4, yo, k 1, p 2, k 1, p 1, p 2 tog, k 1, p 2 tog, p 1, k 1, p 2, k 1, yo, k 4, repeat from * across. **Row 11:** * K 5, yo, k 1, p 2 tog, (k 1, p 2) twice, k 1, p 2 tog, k 1, yo, k 5, repeat from * across. **Row 13:** * K 6, yo, k 1, p 1, k 1, (p 2 tog, k 1) twice, p 1, k 1, yo, k 6, repeat from * across.

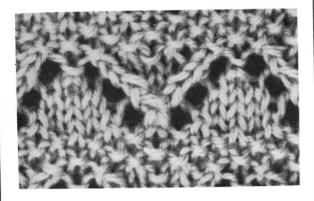

[171]
Multiple of 8 sts plus 1: **Rows 1, 2, 3, and 4:** * K 1, p 1, repeat from * across, and end k 1. **Row 5:** * K 1, yo, sl 1, k 1, psso, k 3, k 2 tog, yo, repeat from * across, and end k 1. **Rows 6, 8, and 10:** P. **Row 7:** * K 2, yo, sl 1, k 1, psso, k 1, k 2 tog, yo, k 1, repeat from * across, and end k 2. **Row 9:** * K 3, yo, sl 1, k 2 tog, psso, yo, k 2, repeat from * across, and end k 3.

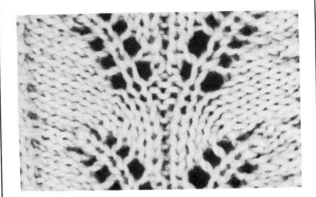

[172]
Multiple of 29 sts: **Row 1:** * K 1, sl 1, k 2 tog, psso, k 9, yo, k 1, yo, p 2, yo, k 1, yo, k 9, sl 1, k 2 tog, psso, repeat from * across. **Rows 2, 4, 6, 8, and 10:** * P 13, k 2, p 14, repeat from * across. **Row 3:** * K 1, sl 1, k 2 tog, psso, k 8, (yo, k 1) twice, p 2, (k 1, yo) twice, k 8, sl 1, k 2 tog, psso, repeat from * across. **Row 5:** * K 1, sl 1, k 2 tog, psso, k 7, yo, k 1, yo, k 2, p 2, k 2, yo, k 1, yo, k 7, sl 1, k 2 tog, psso, repeat from * across. **Row 7:** * K 1, sl 1, k 2 tog, psso, k 6, yo, k 1, yo, k 3, p 2, k 3, yo, k 1, yo, k 6, sl 1, k 2 tog, psso, repeat from * across. **Row 9:** * K 1, sl 1, k 2 tog, psso, k 5, yo, k 1, yo, k 4, p 2, k 4, yo, k 1, yo, k 5, sl 1, k 2 tog, psso, repeat from * across.

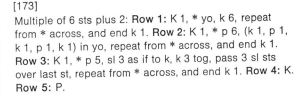

[173]

Multiple of 6 sts plus 2: **Row 1:** K 1, * yo, k 6, repeat from * across, and end k 1. **Row 2:** K 1, * p 6, (k 1, p 1, k 1, p 1, k 1) in yo, repeat from * across, and end k 1. **Row 3:** K 1, * p 5, sl 3 as if to k, k 3 tog, pass 3 sl sts over last st, repeat from * across, and end k 1. **Row 4:** K. **Row 5:** P.

[174]

Multiple of 19 sts plus 2. **Rows 1, 3, 5, and 7:** K 1. * sl 1, k 1, psso, k 3, (yo, sl 1, k 1, psso) twice, yo, k 1, yo, (k 2 tog, yo) twice, k 3, k 2 tog, repeat from * across, and end k 1. **Rows 2, 4, 6, 8, 10, 12, 14, 16, 18, 20, 22, 24, 26, 28, 30, and 32:** P. **Row 9:** K 1, * sl 1, k 1, psso, k 2, (yo, k 2 tog) twice, yo, k 3, yo, (sl 1, k 1, psso, yo) twice, k 2, k 2 tog, repeat from * across, and end k 1. **Row 11:** K 1, * sl 1, k 1, psso, k 1, (yo, k 2 tog) twice, yo, k 5, yo, (sl 1, k 1, psso, yo) twice, k 1, k 2 tog, repeat from * across, and end k 1. **Row 13:** K 1, * sl 1, k 1, psso, (yo, k 2 tog) twice, yo, k 7, yo, (sl 1, k 1, psso, yo) twice, k 2 tog, repeat from * across, and inc 1 st in last st. **Row 15:** Sl 1, * k 1, psso, (yo, k 2 tog) twice, yo, k 3, k 2 tog, k 4, yo, (sl 1, k 1, psso, yo) twice, sl 1, repeat from * across, and end k 1, psso, k 1. **Rows 17, 19, 21, and 23:** K 1, * (yo, k 2 tog) twice, yo, k 3, k 2 tog, sl 1, k 1, psso, k 3, yo, (sl 1, k 1, psso, yo) twice, k 1, repeat from * across, and end k 1. **Row 25:** K 1, * k 1, (yo, sl 1, k 1, psso) twice, yo, k 2, k 2 tog, sl 1, k 1, psso, k 2, (yo, k 2 tog) twice, yo, k 2, repeat from * across, and end k 1. **Row 27:** K 1, * k 2, (yo, sl 1, k 1, psso) twice, yo, k 1, k 2 tog, sl 1, k 1, psso, k 1, yo, (k 2 tog, yo) twice, k 3, repeat from * across, and end k 1. **Row 29:** K 1, * k 3, (yo, sl 1, k 1, psso) twice, yo, k 2 tog, sl 1, k 1, psso, yo, (k 2 tog, yo) twice, k 4, repeat from * across, and end k 1. **Row 31:** K 1, * k 4, (yo, sl 1, k 1, psso) twice, yo, sl 1, k 1, psso, yo, (k 2 tog, yo) twice, k 3, k 2 tog, repeat from * across, and end k 1.

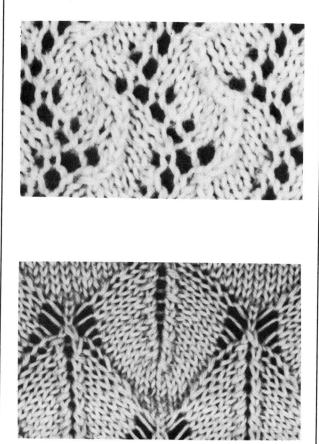

[175]

Multiple of 8 sts: **Row 1:** * Yo, k 1, yo, sl 1, k 1, psso, k 5, repeat from * across. **Row 2:** * P 4, p 2 tog, p 3, repeat from * across. **Row 3:** * Yo, k 1, yo, k 2, sl 1, k 1, psso, k 3, repeat from * across. **Row 4:** * P 2, p 2 tog, p 5, repeat from * across. **Row 5:** * K 1, yo, k 4, sl 1, k 1, psso, k 1, yo, repeat from * across. **Row 6:** * P 1, p 2 tog, p 6, repeat from * across. **Row 7:** * K 5, k 2 tog, yo, k 1, yo, repeat from * across. **Row 8:** * P 3, p 2 tog, p 4, repeat from * across. **Row 9:** * K 3, k 2 tog, k 2, yo, k 1, yo, repeat from * across. **Row 10:** * P 5, p 2 tog, p 2, repeat from * across. **Row 11:** * Yo, k 1, k 2 tog, k 4, yo, k 1, repeat from * across. **Row 12:** * P 6, p 2 tog, p 1, repeat from * across.

[176]

Multiple of 19 sts plus 9: **Row 1:** * Yo, k 7, sl 1, k 1, psso, k 2 tog, k 7, yo, k 1, repeat from * across, and end yo, k 7, sl 1, k 1, psso. **Row 2:** P 2 tog, p 6, yo, p 1, * p 2, yo, p 6, (p 2 tog) twice, p 6, yo, p 1, repeat from * across. **Row 3:** * K 2, yo, k 5, sl 1, k 1, psso, k 2 tog, k 5, yo, k 3, repeat from * across, and end k 2, yo, k 5, sl 1, k 1, psso. **Row 4:** P 2 tog, p 4, yo, p 3, * p 4, yo, p 4, (p 2 tog) twice, p 4, yo, p 3, repeat from * across. **Row 5:** * K 4, yo, k 3, sl 1, k 1, psso, k 2 tog, k 3, yo, k 5, repeat from * across, and end k 4, yo, k 3, sl 1, k 1, psso. **Row 6:** P 2 tog, p 2, yo, p 5, * p 6, yo, p 2, (p 2 tog) twice, p 2, yo, p 5, repeat from * across. **Row 7:** * K 6, yo, k 1, sl 1, k 1, psso, k 2 tog, k 1, yo, k 7, repeat from * across, and end k 6, yo, k 1, sl 1, k 1, psso. **Row 8:** P 2 tog, yo, p 7, * p 8, yo, (p 2 tog) twice, yo, p 7, repeat from * across. **Row 9:** * K 8, yo, sl 1, k 1, psso, yo, k 7, sl 1, k 1, psso, repeat from * across, and end k 8, yo, k 1. **Row 10:** P 1, yo, p 7, p 2 tog, * p 2 tog, p 7, yo, p 1, yo, p 7, p 2 tog, repeat from * across. **Row 11:** * K 2 tog, k 7, yo, k 1, yo, k 7, sl 1, k 1, psso, repeat from * across, and end k 2 tog, k 7, yo, k 1. **Row 12:** P 2, yo, p 6, p 2 tog,* p 2 tog, p 6, yo, p 3, yo, p 6, p 2 tog, repeat from * across. **Row 13:** * K 2 tog, k 5, (yo, k 5) twice, sl 1, k 1, psso, repeat from * across, and end k 2 tog, k 5, yo, k 3. **Row 14:** P 4, yo, p 4, p 2 tog, * p 2 tog, p 4, yo, p 7, yo, p 4, p 2 tog, repeat from * across. **Row 15:** * K 2 tog, k 3, yo, k 9, yo, k 3, sl 1, k 1, psso, repeat from * across, and end k 2 tog, k 3, yo, k 5, **Row 16:** P 6, yo, p 2, p 2 tog, * p 2 tog, p 2, yo, p 11, yo, p 2, p 2 tog, repeat from * across. **Row 17:** * K 2 tog, k 1, yo, k 13, yo, k 1, sl 1, k 1, psso, repeat from * across, and end k 2 tog, k 1, yo, k 7. **Row 18:** P 8, yo, p 2 tog, * p 2 tog, yo, p 15, yo, p 2 tog, repeat from * across. **Row 19:** Yo, k 1, pass yo over, * yo, k 7, sl 1, k 1, psso, k 8, yo, sl 1, k 1, psso, repeat from * across, and end yo, k 7, sl 1, k 1, psso. **Row 20:** P 2 tog, p 7, * yo, p 1, yo, p 7, (p 2 tog) twice, p 7, repeat from * across, and end p 8.

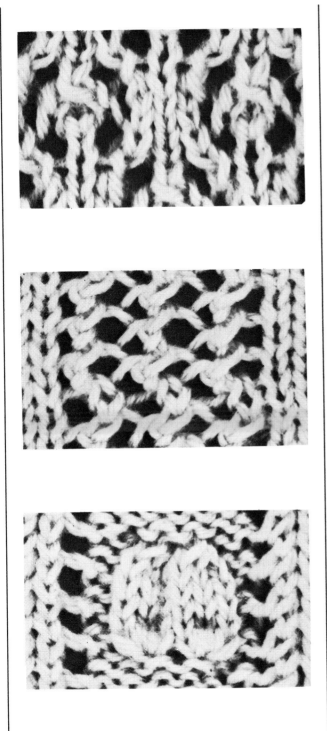

[177]

Multiple of 6 sts plus 1: **Row 1:** * K 1, yo, sl 1, k 1, psso, k 1, k 2 tog, yo, repeat from * across, and end k 1. **Rows 2, 4, 6, 8, 10, and 12:** P. **Rows 3 and 9:** * K 2, yo, k 3, yo, k 1, repeat from * across, and end k 2. **Row 5:** K 2 tog, * yo, sl 1, k 1, psso, k 1, k 2 tog, yo, sl 1, k 2 tog, psso, repeat from * across, and end sl 1, k 1, psso. **Row 7:** * K 1, k 2 tog, yo, k 1, yo, sl 1, k 1, psso, repeat from * across, and end k 1. **Row 11:** * K 1, k 2 tog, yo, sl 1, k 2 tog, psso, yo, sl 1, k 1, psso, repeat from * across, and end k 1.

[178]

Multiple of 12 sts plus 6: **Rows 1, 3, 5, and 7:** * K 6, (k 2 tog, yo) 3 times, repeat from * across, and end k 6. **Rows 2, 4, and 6:** * P 6 (p 2 tog, yo) 3 times, repeat from * across, and end p 6. **Row 8:** P.

[179]

Multiple of 10 sts plus 4: **Rows 1 and 9 (wrong side):** P 4, * k 6, p 4, repeat from * across. **Row 2:** * Yo, (k 2 tog) twice, yo, p 2, (k 1, p 1, k 1 in next st) twice, p 2, repeat from * across, and end yo, (k 2 tog) twice, yo. **Rows 3, 5, and 7:** P 4, * k 2, p 6, k 2, p 4, repeat from * across. **Rows 4 and 6:** * Yo, (k 2 tog) twice, yo, p 2, k 6, p 2, repeat from * across, and end yo, (k 2 tog) twice, yo. **Row 8:** * Yo, (k 2 tog) twice, yo, p 2, (k 3 tog) twice, p 2, repeat from * across, and end yo, (k 2 tog) twice, yo. **Row 10:** * Yo, (k 2 tog) twice, yo, p 6, repeat from * across, and end yo, (k 2 tog) twice, yo.

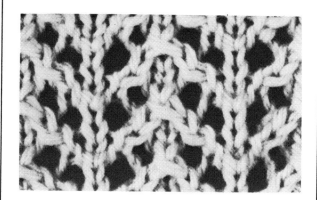

[180]
Multiple of 6 sts plus 3: **Row 1:** K 2, * yo, sl 1, k 1, psso, k 1, k 2 tog, yo, k 1, repeat from * across, and end yo, k 2. **Rows 2 and 4:** P. **Row 3:** K 3, * yo, sl 1, k 2 tog, psso, yo, k 3, repeat from * across.

[181]
Multiple of 14 sts plus 1: **Row 1 (wrong side).** P 1, * k 4, p 5, k 4, p 1, repeat from * across. **Row 2:** K 1, * p 4, yo, k 2 tog, yo, k 1, yo, k 2 tog, yo, p 4, k 1, repeat from * across. **Row 3:** P 1, * k 4, p 7, k 4, p 1, repeat from * across. **Row 4:** K 1, * p 4, yo, k 2 tog, yo, k 3, yo, k 2 tog, yo, p 4, k 1, repeat from * across. **Rows 5 and 7:** P 1, * k 4, p 9, k 4, p 1, repeat from * across. **Row 6:** K 1, * p 4, yo, k 2 tog, yo, k 2 tog, k 1, k 2 tog, yo, k 2 tog, yo, p 4, k 1, repeat from * across. **Row 8:** K 1, * p 4, yo, (k 2 tog) twice, k 3 tog, pass 2nd st on right-hand needle over 1st st on right-hand needle, k 2 tog, yo, p 4, k 1, repeat from * across.

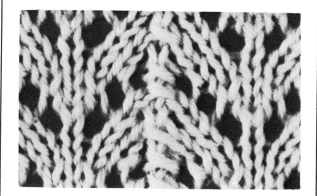

[182]
Multiple of 8 sts plus 1: **Row 1:** * K 1, yo, k 2, sl 1, k 2 tog, psso, k 2, yo, repeat from * across, and end k 1. **Rows 2, 4, and 6:** P. **Row 3:** * K 2, yo, k 1, sl 1, k 2 tog, psso, k 1, yo, k 1, repeat from * across, and end k 2. **Row 5:** * K 3, yo, sl 1, k 2 tog, psso, yo, k 2, repeat from * across, and end k 3.

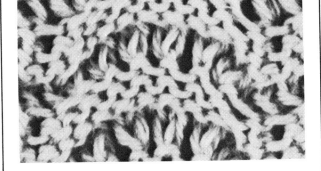

[183]
Multiple of 16 sts: **Row 1:** K 4, * yo twice, k 1, repeat from * across, and end k 5. **Row 2:** K 5, * drop 1 yo, p 2, repeat from * across, and end drop 1 yo, p 1, k **4. Row 3:** K 4, * k 2 tog, k 12, k 2 tog, repeat from * across, and end k 4. **Row 4:** K 4,* k 2 tog, k 10, k 2 tog, repeat from * across, and end k 4. **Row 5:** K 4, * p 2 tog, p 8, p 2 tog, repeat from * across, and end k 4. **Row 6:** K 4, * k 2 tog, k 6, k 2 tog, repeat from * across, and end k 4.

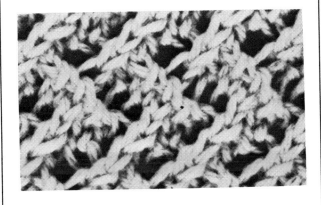

[184]
Multiple of 4 sts plus 2: **Row 1:** K 1, * yo, k 2 tog, k 2, repeat from * across, and end k 3. **Row 2:** P 2, * p 2 tog, yo, p 2, repeat from * across. **Row 3:** K 3, * yo, k 2 tog, k 2, repeat from * across, and end k 1. **Row 4:** * P 2 tog, yo, p 2, repeat from * across, and end p 4. **Row 5:** K 3, * k 2 tog, yo, k 2, repeat from * across, and end k 1.
Row 6: * P 2, yo, p 2 tog, repeat from * across, and end p 2. **Row 7:** K 1, * k 2 tog, yo, k 2, repeat from * across, and end k 3. **Row 8:** P 4, * yo, p 2 tog, p 2, repeat from * across, and end yo, p 2 tog.

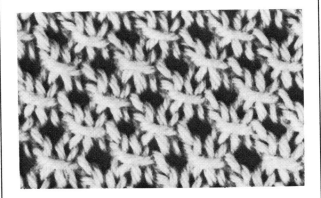

[185]
Multiple of 3 sts plus 2: **Row 1:** K 2, * yo, k 3, pass 1st st over next 2 sts, repeat from * across. **Rows 2, 4, and 6:** P. **Row 3:** K 1, * yo, k 3, pass 1st st over next 2 sts, repeat from * across, and end k 1. **Row 5:** K 3, * yo, k 3, pass 1st st over next 2 sts, repeat from * across, and end k 2.

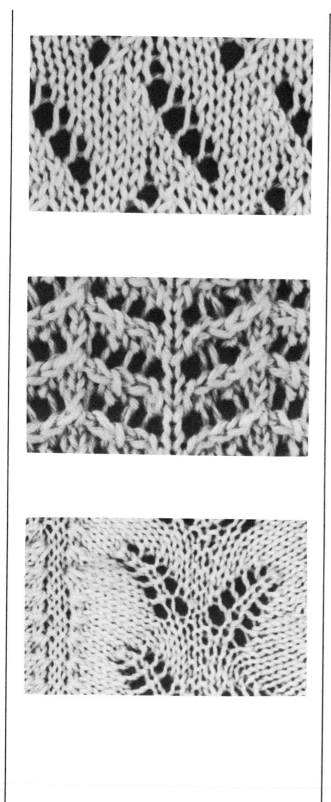

[186]
Multiple of 7 sts: Row 1: * K 5, k 2 tog, yo, repeat from * across. Rows 2, 4, 6, 8, 10, 12, 14, and 16: P. Row 3: * K 4, k 2 tog, yo, k 1, repeat from * across. Row 5: * K 3, k 2 tog, yo, k 2, repeat from * across. Row 7: * K 2, k 2 tog, yo, k 3, repeat from * across. Row 9: * Yo, k 2 tog, k 5, repeat from * across. Row 11: * K 1, yo, k 2 tog, k 4, repeat from * across. Row 13: * K 2, yo, k 2 tog, k 3, repeat from * across. Row 15: * K 3, yo, k 2 tog, k 2, repeat from * across.

[187]
Multiple of 10 sts plus 3: Row 1: K 2, * yo, sl 1, k 1, psso, k 5, k 2 tog, yo, k 1, repeat from * across, and end k 2. Row 2: P 3, * yo, p 2 tog, p 3, p 2 tog, yo, p 3, repeat from * across. Row 3: K 4, * yo, sl 1, k 1, psso, k 1, k 2 tog, yo, k 5, repeat from * across, and end k 4. Row 4: P 5, * yo, p 3 tog, yo, p 7, repeat from * across, and end p 5.

[188]
Multiple of 30 sts: Row 1: * P 1, k 3 tog, k 9, yo, k 1, yo, p 2, yo, k 1, yo, k 9, sl 1 as if to p, k 2 tog, psso, p 1, repeat from * across. Rows 2, 4, 6, 8, and 10: P. Row 3: * P 1, k 3 tog, k 8, yo, k 1, yo, k 1, p 2, k 1, yo, k 1, yo, k 8, sl 1, k 2 tog, psso, p 1, repeat from * across. Row 5: * P 1, k 3 tog, k 7, yo, k 1, yo, k 2, p 2, k 2, yo, k 1, yo, k 7, sl 1, k 2 tog, psso, p 1, repeat from * across. Row 7: * P 1, k 3 tog, k 6, yo, k 1, yo, k 3, p 2, k 3, yo, k 1, yo, k 6, sl 1, k 2 tog, psso, p 1, repeat from * across. Row 9: * P 1, k 3 tog, k 5, yo, k 1, yo, k 4, p 2, k 4, yo, k 1, yo, k 5, sl 1, k 2 tog, psso, p 1, repeat from * across.

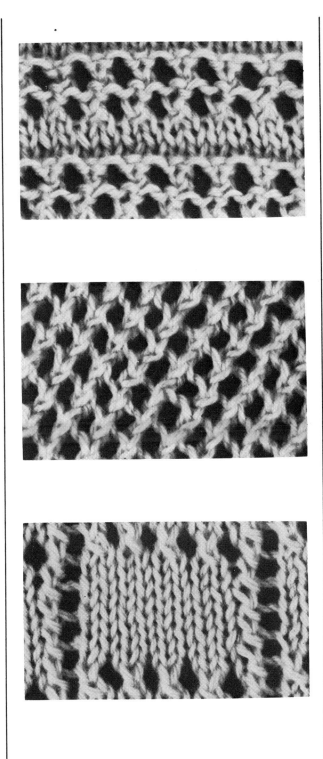

[189]
Multiple of 2 sts: **Rows 1 and 3:** K. **Rows 2 and 4:** P.
Rows 5 and 7: * Yo, p 2 tog, repeat from * across. **Rows 6 and 8:** K.

[190]
Multiple of 2 sts plus 1: **Row 1 (wrong side):** K 2, * yo, k 2 tog, repeat from * across, and end k 1. **Rows 2 and 4:** K. **Row 3:** K 1, * yo, k 2 tog, repeat from * across, and end k 2.

[191]
Multiple of 10 sts plus 8: **Row 1:** * Yo, sl 1, k 1, psso, repeat from * across. **Rows 2, 4, 6, 8, and 10:** P. **Rows 3, 5, 7, and 9:** * K 8, yo, sl 1, k 1, psso, repeat from * across, and end k 8.

[192]

Multiple of 11 sts plus 5: **Row 1:** * K 3, (yo, sl 1, k 1, psso) 4 times, repeat from * across, and end k 5. **Rows 2, 4, 6, 8, and 10:** P. **Row 3:** * K 4, (yo, sl 1, k 1, psso) 3 times, k 1, repeat from * across and end k 6. **Row 5:** * K 5, (yo, sl 1, k 1, psso) twice, k 2, repeat from * across, and end k 7. **Row 7:** * K 6, yo, sl 1, k 1, psso, k 3, repeat from * across, and end k 8. **Row 9:** K 5, * k 3, (yo, sl 1, k 1, psso) 4 times, repeat from * across.

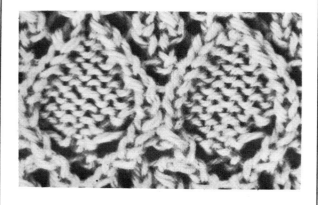

[193]

Multiple of 8 sts plus 2: **Rows 1 and 3:** K 1, p 3, * k 2, p 6, repeat from * across, and end k 2, p 3, k 1. **Rows 2 and 4:** K 4, p 2, * k 6, p 2, repeat from * across, and end k 4. **Row 5:** K 1, p 2, * k 2 tog, yo, sl 1, k 1, psso, p 4, repeat from * across, and end k 2 tog, yo, sl 1, k 1, psso, p 3. **Row 6:** K 3, * p 1, k into front and back of next st, p 1, k 4, repeat from * across, and end k 3. **Row 7:** K 1, p 1, * k 2 tog, yo, k 2, yo, sl 1, k 1, psso, p 2, repeat from * across. **Row 8:** K 2, * p 6, k 2, repeat from * across. **Row 9:** K 1, * k 2 tog, yo, k 2 tog, yo, sl 1, k 1, psso, yo, sl 1, k 1, psso, repeat from * across, and end k 1. **Row 10:** K 1, p 3, * k into front and back of next st, p 6, repeat from * across, and end p 4. **Row 11:** K 1, * yo, sl 1, k 1, psso, yo, sl 1, k 1, psso, k 2 tog, yo, k 2 tog, repeat from * across, and end yo, k 1. **Row 12:** K 2, p 6, * k into front and back of next st, p 6, repeat from * across, and end k 2. **Row 13:** K 1, p 1,* yo, sl 1 as if to p, k 2 tog, psso, yo, k 3 tog, yo, p 2, repeat from * across. **Row 14:** K 2, * k 1, p 1, k into front and back of next st, p 1, k 3, repeat from * across. **Row 15:** K 1, p 2, * yo, sl 1 as if to p, k 1, psso, k 2 tog, yo, p 4, repeat from * across, and end p 2, k 1. **Row 16:** K 3, * k 1, p 2, k 5, repeat from * across, and end k 4. Repeat rows 3 through 16 for pattern.

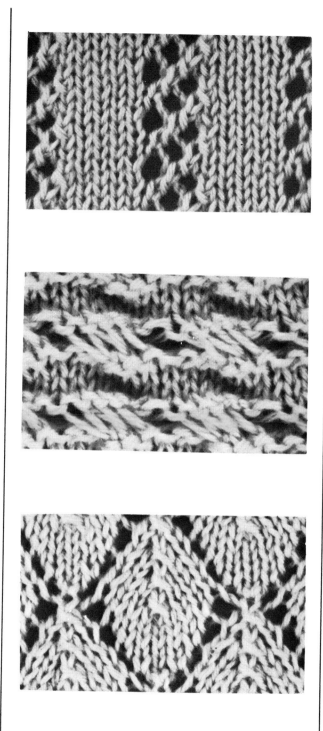

[194]

Multiple of 8 sts plus 1: **Row 1:** K 2, * sl 1, k 1, psso, yo, sl 1, k 1, psso, yo, k 4, repeat from * across, and end k 3. **Rows 2 and 4:** P. **Row 3:** K 3, * sl 1, k 1, psso, yo, k 6, repeat from * across, and end k 4.

[195]

Multiple of 6 sts: **Row 1:** K, wrapping yarn twice around for each st. **Row 2:** * Sl 3 on dp needle (dropping extra lps), hold in front, k 3 (dropping extra lps), k 3 from dp needle, repeat from * across. **Rows 3, 5, and 6:** K. **Row 4:** P.

[196]

Multiple of 10 sts plus 6: **Row 1:** K 1, yo, * k 3, sl 1, k 2 tog, psso, k 3, yo, k 1, yo, repeat from * across, and end k 3, sl 1, k 1, psso. **Rows 2, 4, 6, 8, 10, 12, 14, and 16:** P. **Row 3:** K 2, yo, * k 2, sl 1, k 2 tog, psso, k 2, yo, k 3, yo, repeat from * across, and end k 2, sl 1, k 1, psso. **Row 5:** K 3, yo, * k 1, sl 1, k 2 tog, psso, k 1, yo, k 5, yo, repeat from * across, and end k 1, sl 1, k 1, psso. **Row 7:** K 4, yo, * sl 1, k 2 tog, psso, yo, k 7, yo, repeat from * across, and end sl 1, k 1, psso. **Row 9:** Sl 1, k 1, psso, k 3, yo, * k 1, yo, k 3, sl 1, k 2 tog, psso, k 3, yo, repeat from * across, and end k 1. **Row 11:** Sl 1, k 1, psso, k 2, yo, k 1, * k 2, yo, k 2, sl 1, k 2 tog, psso, k 2, yo, k 1, repeat from * across, and end k 2. **Row 13:** Sl 1, k 1, psso, k 1, yo, k 2, * k 3, yo, k 1, sl 1, k 2 tog, psso, k 1, yo, k 2, repeat from * across, and end k 3. **Row 15:** Sl 1, k 1, psso, yo, k 3, * k 4, yo, sl 1, k 2 tog, psso, yo, k 3, repeat from * across, and end k 4.

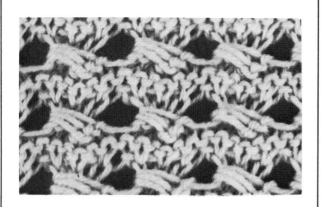

[197]

Multiple of 6 sts: **Rows 1 and 4:** K. **Row 2:** K, wrapping yarn twice around for each st. **Row 3:** * Sl 6 (dropping extra lps), pass 1st 3 sts over 2nd 3 sts, sl remaining 3 sts back onto left-hand needle, k into front and back of 3 sts, repeat from * across.

[198]

Multiple of 5 sts plus 2: **Rows 1 and 5:** K 2, * yo, k 1, repeat from * across, and end k 2. **Rows 2 and 6:** P 2, * drop yo, p 1, repeat from * across, and end p 2. **Row 3:** K 1, * sl 2, k 2 tog, pass 2 sl sts over last st, (k 1, p 1, k 1, p 1) in next st, repeat from * across, and end k 1. **Rows 4 and 8:** P. **Row 7:** K 1, * (k 1, p 1, k 1, p 1) in next st, sl 2, k 2 tog, pass 2 sl sts over last st, repeat from * across, and end k 1.

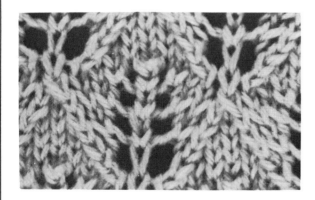

[199]

Multiple of 10 sts plus 6: **Row 1:** K 3, * k 2 tog, yo, k 1, yo, sl 1, k 1, psso, k 5, repeat from * across, and end k 2 tog, yo, k 1. **Rows 2, 4, 6, 8, 10, 12, 14, and 16:** P. **Row 3:** K 2, * k 2 tog, k 1, yo, k 1, yo, k 1, sl 1, k 1, psso, k 3, repeat from * across, and end k 2 tog, k 1, yo, k 1. **Row 5:** K 1, * k 2 tog, k 2, yo, k 1, yo, k 2, sl 1, k 1, psso, k 1, repeat from * across, and end k 2 tog, k 2, yo, k 1. **Row 7:** K 2 tog, * k 3, yo, k 1, yo, k 3, sl 1, k 2 tog, psso, repeat from * across, and end k 3, yo, k 1. **Row 9:** K 1, * yo, sl 1, k 1, psso, k 5, k 2 tog, yo, k 1, repeat from * across, and end yo, sl 1, k 1, psso, k 3. **Row 11:** K 1, * yo, k 1, sl 1, k 1, psso, k 3, k 2 tog, k 1, yo, k 1, repeat from * across, and end yo, k 1, sl 1, k 1, psso, k 2. **Row 13:** K 1, * yo, k 2, sl 1, k 1, psso, k 1, k 2 tog, k 2, yo, k 1, repeat from * across, and end yo, k 2, sl 1, k 1, psso, k 1. **Row 15:** K 1, * yo, k 3, sl 1, k 2 tog, psso, k 3, yo, k 1, repeat from * across, and end yo, k 3, sl 1, k 1, psso.

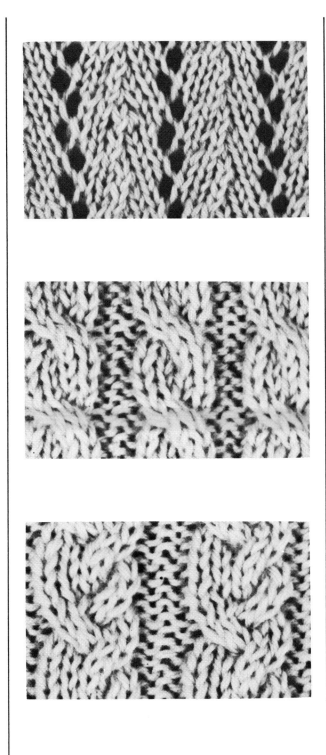

[200]
Multiple of 6 sts: **Row 1:** * Yo, k 2, k 2 tog, k 2, repeat from * across. **Rows 2 and 4:** P. **Row 3:** * K 2, k 2 tog, k 2, yo, repeat from * across.

[201]
Multiple of 7 sts plus 3: **Rows 1 and 3:** * P 3, k 4, repeat from * across, and end p 3. **Rows 2, 4, and 6:** * K 3, p 4, repeat from * across, and end k 3. **Row 5:** * P 3, sl 2 on dp needle, hold in front, k 2, k 2 from dp needle, repeat from * across, and end p 3.

[202]
Multiple of 9 sts plus 3: **Row 1:** * P 3, k 6, repeat from * across, and end p 3. **Rows 2, 4, 6, and 8:** * K 3, p 6, repeat from * across, and end k 3. **Rows 3 and 7:** * P 3, sl 2 on dp needle, hold in back, k 2, k 2 from dp needle, k 2, repeat from * across, and end p 3. **Row 5:** * P 3, k 2, sl 2 on dp needle, hold in front, k 2, k 2 from dp needle, repeat from * across, and end p 3.

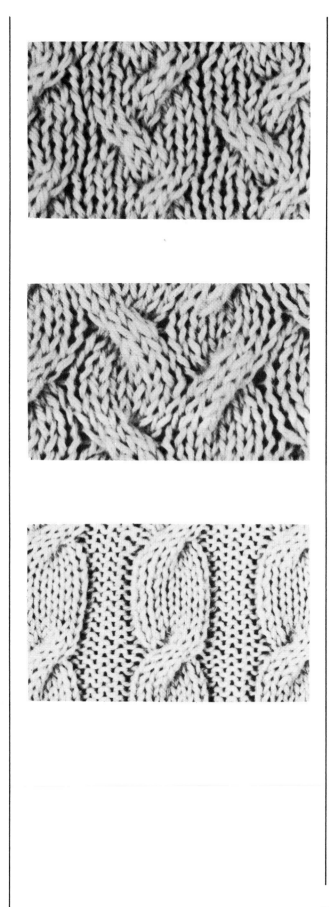

[203]
Multiple of 7 sts: **Rows 1 and 5:** K. **Rows 2, 4, 6, and 8:** P. **Row 3:** * Sl 2 on dp needle, hold in back, k 2, k 2 from dp needle, k 3, repeat from * across. **Row 7:** * K 2, sl 2 on dp needle, hold in front, k 2, k 2 from dp needle, k 1, repeat from * across.

[204]
Multiple of 12 sts: **Rows 1, 5, and 9:** K. **Rows 2, 4, 6, and 8:** P. **Row 3:** * Sl 3 on dp needle, hold in front, k 3, k 3 from dp needle, k 6, repeat from * across. **Row 7:** * K 6, sl 3 on dp needle, hold in back, k 3, k 3 from dp needle, repeat from * across. Repeat rows 3 through 8 for pattern.

[205]
Multiple of 11 sts plus 5: **Rows 1, 3, 5, 7, and 9:** P 5, * k 6, p 5, repeat from * across. **Rows 2, 4, 6, 8, 10, and 12:** K 5, * p 6, k 5, repeat from * across. **Row 11:** P 5, * sl 3 on dp needle, hold in back, k 3, k 3 from dp needle, p 5, repeat from * across.

[206]
Multiple of 12 sts plus 3: **Rows 1, 5, and 9:** * P 3, k 9, repeat from * across, and end p 3. **Rows 2, 4, 6, 8, and 10:** * K 3, p 9, repeat from * across, and end k 3. **Row 3:** * P 3, sl 3 on dp needle, hold in back, k 3, k 3 from dp needle, k 3, repeat from * across, and end p 3. **Row 7:** * P 3, k 3, sl 3 on dp needle, hold in front, k 3, k 3 from dp needle, repeat from * across, and end p 3. Repeat rows 3 through 10 for pattern.

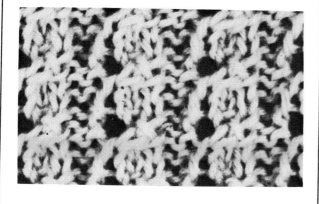

[207]
Multiple of 5 sts plus 2: **Row 1:** P 2, * sl 1 as if to p, k 2 tog, psso, yo twice, p 2, repeat from * across. **Row 2:** * K 2, p in front and back of double yo, p 1, repeat from * across, and end k 2. **Row 3:** P 2, * k 3, p 2, repeat from * across. **Row 4:** * K 2, p 3, repeat from * across, and end k 2.

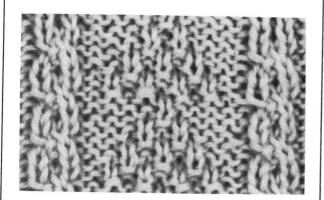

[208]
Multiple of 14 sts: **Row 1:** * P 1, k 1, p 1, k 1, p 2, sl 2 on dp needle, hold in front, k 1, k 2 from dp needle, p 2, k 1, p 1, k 1, repeat from * across. **Rows 2, 4, 6, and 8:** K the p sts and p the k sts of previous row. **Row 3:** * K 1, p 1, k 1, p 3, k 1, p 1, k 1, p 3, k 1, p 1, repeat from * across. **Row 5:** * P 1, k 1, p 4, sl 2 on dp needle, hold in front, k 1, k 2 from dp needle, p 4, k 1, repeat from * across. **Row 7:** * K 1, p 5, k 1, p 1, k 1, p 5, repeat from * across.

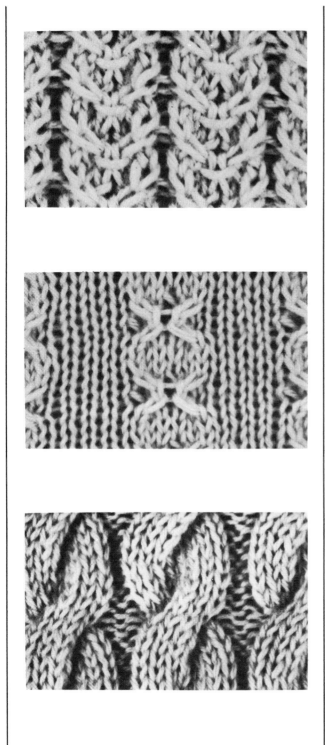

[209]
Multiple of 7 sts plus 1: **Row 1:** P. **Row 2:** K 1, * p 6, k 1, repeat from * across. **Row 3:** P 1, * k 2, sl 2 as if to p, k 2, p 1, repeat from * across. **Row 4:** K 1, * p 2, sl 2, p 2, k 1, repeat from * across. **Row 5:** P 1, * sl 2 on dp needle, hold in back, k 1, k 2 from dp needle, sl 1 on dp needle, hold in front, k 2, k 1 from dp needle, p 1, repeat from * across. Repeat rows 2 through 5 for pattern.

[210]
Multiple of 10 sts: **Row 1:** * K 2, sl 1 on dp needle, hold in front, k 2, k 1 from dp needle, sl 2 on dp needle, hold in back, k 1, k 2 from dp needle, k 2, repeat from * across. **Rows 2, 4, and 6:** P. **Row 3:** * K 2, sl 2 on dp needle, hold in back, k 1, k 2 from dp needle, sl 1 on dp needle, hold in front, k 2, k 1 from dp needle, k 2, repeat from * across. **Row 5:** K.

[211]
Multiple of 10 sts: **Rows 1, 3, 7, and 9:** * P 1, k 8, p 1, repeat from * across. **Rows 2, 4, 6, 8, and 10:** * K 1, p 8, k 1, repeat from * across. **Row 5:** * P 1, sl 4 on dp needle, hold in back, k 4, k 4 from dp needle, p 1, repeat from * across.

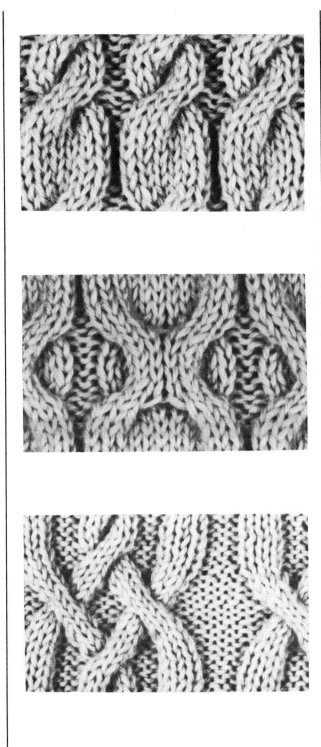

[212]
Multiple of 8 sts: **Rows 1, 3, 7, 9, 11, and 13:** * P 1, k 6, p 1, repeat from * across. **Rows 2, 4, 6, 8, 10, 12, 14, and 16:** * K 1, p 6, k 1, repeat from * across. **Rows 5 and 15:** * P 1, sl 3 on dp needle, hold in back, k 3, k 3 from dp needle, p 1, repeat from * across.

[213]
Multiple of 14 sts plus 2: **Row 1:** P 2, * sl 3 on dp needle, hold in back, k 3, k 3 from dp needle (back cable), sl 3 on dp needle, hold in front, k 3, k 3 from dp needle (front cable), p 2, repeat from * across. **Rows 2, 4, 6, 8, 10, 12, 14, and 16:** K 2, * p 12, k 2, repeat from * across. **Rows 3, 5, 7, 9, 13, and 15:** P 2, * k 12, p 2, repeat from * across. **Row 11:** P 2, * front cable, back cable, p 2, repeat from * across.

[214]
Multiple of 24 sts plus 4: **Rows 1 and 7:** P 4, * k 3, p 4, sl 3 on dp needle, hold in back, k 3, k 3 from dp needle (right cable), p 4, k 3, p 4, repeat from * across. **Rows 2, 4, 6, and 8:** K 4, * p 3, k 4, p 6, k 4, p 3, k 4, repeat from * across. **Rows 3 and 5:** P 4, * k 3, p 4, k 6, p 4, k 3, p 4, repeat from * across. **Row 9:** P 4, * sl 3 on dp needle, hold in front, p 1, k 3 from dp needle (left twist), p 2, sl 1 on dp needle, hold in back, k 3, p 1 from dp needle (right twist), left twist, p 2, right twist, p 4, repeat from * across. **Rows 10 and 16:** K 5, * p 3, (k 2, p 3) 3 times, k 5, repeat from * across. **Row 11:** P 5, * left twist, right twist, p 2, left twist, right twist, p 5, repeat from * across. **Rows 12 and 14:** K 6, * p 6, k 4, p 6, k 6, repeat from * across. **Row 13:** P 6, * sl 3 on dp needle, hold in front, k 3, k 3 from dp needle (left cable), p 4, left cable, p 6, repeat from * across. **Row 15:** P 5, * right twist, left twist, p 2, right twist, left twist, p 5, repeat from * across. **Row 17:** P 4, * right twist, p 2, left twist, right twist, p 2, left twist, p 4, repeat from * across. **Row 18:** K 4, * p 3, k 4, p 6, k 4, p 3, k 4, repeat from * across.

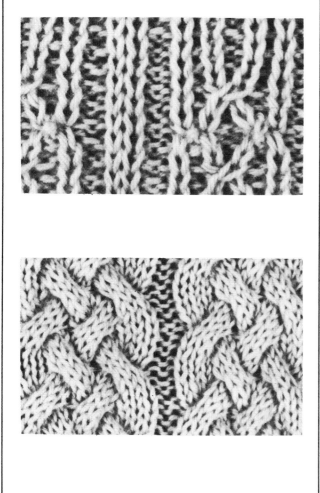

[215]

Multiple of 14 sts plus 6: **Rows 1, 3, 5, 9, 13, 17, 19, 21, and 23:** P 2, sl 2 as if to k, * (p 2, sl 1 as if to k, p 1, sl 1 as if to k) twice, p 2, sl 2 as if to k, repeat from * across, and end p 2. **Rows 2, 4, 6, 8, 10, 12, 14, 16, 18, 20, 22, and 24:** K 2, p 2, * (k 2, p 1, k 1, p 1) twice, k 2, p 2, repeat from * across, and end k 2. **Rows 7 and 15:** P 2, sl 2 as if to k, * p 2, sl 1 as if to k, p 1, sl 3 on dp needle, hold in back, k 1, place 2 sts from dp needle back on left-hand needle, hold dp needle in front, p 2, k 1 from dp needle, p 1, sl 1 as if to k, p 2, sl 2 as if to k, repeat from * across, and end p 2. **Row 11:** P 2, sl 2 as if to k, * p 2, (sl 2 on dp needle, hold in front, k 1, p the 2nd st on dp needle, k the 1st st and drop both sts from dp needle, p 2) twice, sl 2 as if to k, repeat from * across, and end p 2.

[216]

Multiple of 17 sts plus 2: **Rows 1 and 5:** * P 2, k 15, repeat from * across, and end p 2. **Rows 2, 4, 6, and 8:** K 2, * p 15, k 2, repeat from * across. **Row 3:** * P 2, (sl 3 on dp needle, hold in front, k 3, k 3 from dp needle) twice, k 3, repeat from * across, and end p 2. **Row 7:** * P 2, k 3, (sl 3 on dp needle, hold in back, k 3, k 3 from dp needle) twice, repeat from * across, and end p 2.

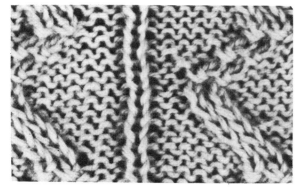

[217]

Multiple of 14 sts: **Row 1:** * K 1, p 7, k the 2nd st on left-hand needle through back lp, p the 1st st and drop both sts from left-hand needle (right twist), right twist, p 2, repeat from * across. **Row 2:** * K 3, (right twist) twice, k 6, p 1, repeat from * across. **Row 3:** * K 1, p 5, (right twist) twice, p 4, repeat from * across. **Row 4:** * K 5, (right twist) twice, k 4, p 1, repeat from * across. **Row 5:** * K 1, p 3, (right twist) twice, p 6, repeat from * across. **Row 6:** * K 7, (right twist) twice, k 2, p 1, repeat from * across. **Row 7:** * K 1, p 2, sl 1 on dp needle, hold in front, p 1, k 1 from dp needle (left twist), left twist, p 7, repeat from * across. **Row 8:** * K 6, (left twist) twice, k 3, p 1, repeat from * across. **Row 9:** * K 1, p 4, (left twist) twice, p 5, repeat from * across. **Row 10:** * K 4, (left twist) twice, k 5, p 1, repeat from * across. **Row 11:** * K 1, p 6, (left twist) twice, p 3, repeat from * across. **Row 12:** * K 2, (left twist) twice, k 7, p 1, repeat from * across.

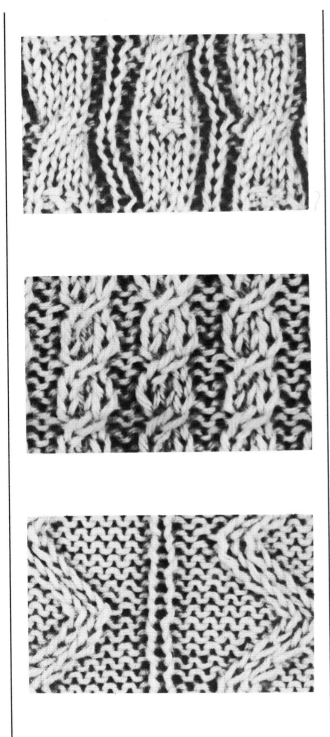

[218]
Multiple of 32 sts. **Row 1 (wrong side):** * K 1, p 2, sl 6 on dp needle, hold in back, k 2, (p 4, k 2) from dp needle (8 st cable), p 1, k 2, p 1, (k 2 turn, p 2, turn) 3 times, (insert needle in 1st st on left-hand needle and in same st 6 rows below, k sts tog) twice (popcorn made), p 1, k 2, p 1, 8 st cable, p 2, k 1, repeat from * across. **Rows 2, 4, 6, 8, 10, and 12:** * P 1, k 2, (p 2, k 4, p 2, k 1) 3 times, k 1, p 1, repeat from * across. **Rows 3, 5, 9, and 11:** * K 1, p 2, (k 2, p 4, k 2, p 1) 3 times, p 1, k 1, repeat from * across. **Row 7:** * K 1, p 2, p 1, popcorn, p 1, k 2, p 1, 8 st cable, p 1, k 2, p 1, popcorn, p 1, k 2, p 2, k 1, repeat from * across.

[219]
Multiple of 5 sts: **Row 1:** P 1, * k the 3rd st on left-hand needle through front lp, k the 1st and 2nd sts and drop 3 sts from left-hand needle (mock cable), p 2, repeat from * across, and end mock cable, p 6. **Rows 2 and 4:** K 1, * p 3, k 2, repeat from * across, and end k 1. **Row 3:** P 1, * k 3, p 2, repeat from * across, and end p 1.

[220]
Multiple of 14 sts: **Row 1:** * P 2, (sl 1 on dp needle, hold in front, p 1, k 1 from dp needle—left twist) twice, p 7, k 1, repeat from * across. **Row 2:** * P 1, k 6, (left twist) twice, k 3, repeat from * across. **Row 3:** * P 4, (left twist) twice, p 5, k 1, repeat from * across. **Row 4:** * P 1, k 4, (left twist) twice, k 5, repeat from * across. **Row 5:** * P 6, (left twist) twice, p 3, k 1, repeat from * across. **Row 6:** * P 1, k 2, (left twist) twice, k 7, repeat from * across. **Row 7:** * P 7, (k the 2nd st on left-hand needle through front lp, p the 1st st and drop both sts from left-hand needle—right twist) twice, p 2, k 1, repeat from * across. **Row 8:** * P 1, k 3, (right twist) twice, k 6, repeat from * across. **Row 9:** * P 5, (right twist) twice, p 4, k 1, repeat from * across. **Row 10:** * P 1, k 5, (right twist) twice, k 4, repeat from * across. **Row 11:** * P 3, (right twist) twice, p 6, k 1, repeat from * across. **Row 12:** * P 1, k 7, (right twist) twice, k 2, repeat from * across.

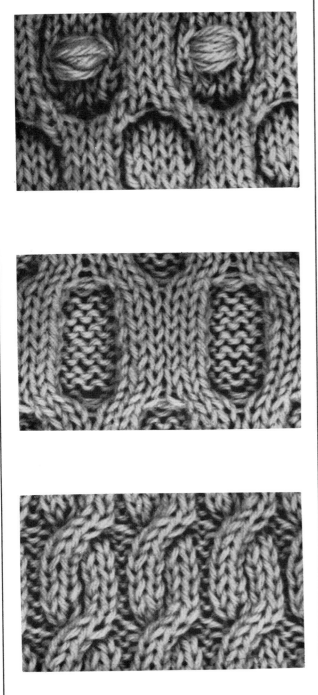

[221]

Multiple of 12 sts: **Rows 1, 3, 7, 9, 11, and 15:** * K 2, p 2, k 4, p 2, k 2, repeat from * across. **Rows 2, 4, 6, 8, 10, 12, 14, 16, and 18:** * P 2, k 2, p 4, k 2, p 2, repeat from * across. **Row 5:** * Sl 3 on dp needle, hold in front, k 2, p 1, (p 1, k 2) from dp needle, sl 3 on dp needle, hold in back, k 2, p 1, (p 1, k 2) from dp needle, repeat from * across. **Row 13:** * Sl 3 on dp needle, hold in back, k 2, p 1, (p 1, k 2) from dp needle, sl 3 on dp needle, hold in front, k 2, p 1, (p 1, k 2) from dp needle, repeat from * across. **Row 17:** * K 2, p 2, k 1, sl 2 on dp needle, wrap yarn 10 times around 2 sts on dp needle, sl 2 sts from dp needle to right-hand needle, k 1, p 2, k 2, repeat from * across.

[222]

Multiple of 12 sts: **Rows 1, 3, 5, and 7:** * K 3, p 6, k 3, repeat from * across. **Rows 2, 4, 6, and 8:** * P 3, k 6, p 3, repeat from * across. **Row 9:** * Sl 3 on dp needle, hold in front, p 3, k 3 from dp needle, sl 3 on dp needle, hold in back, k 3, p 3 from dp needle, repeat from * across. **Rows 10, 12, 14, 16, 18, and 20:** * K 3, p 6, k 3, repeat from * across. **Rows 11, 13, 15, and 17:** * P 3, k 6, p 3, repeat from * across. **Row 19:** * Sl 3 on dp needle, hold in back, k 3, p 3 from dp needle, sl 3 on dp needle, hold in front, p 3, k 3 from dp needle, repeat from * across.

[223]

Multiple of 4 sts plus 2: **Rows 1, 3, 5, and 7 (wrong side):** * K 2, p 2, repeat from * across, and end k 2. **Rows 2, 4, and 6:** * P 2, k 2, repeat from * across, and end p 2. **Row 8:** * P 2, sl 4 on dp needle, hold in back, k 2, sl 2 from dp needle onto left-hand needle, p these 2 sts, k 2 from dp needle, repeat from * across, and end p 2.

[224]

Multiple of 14 sts plus 2: **Row 1 (wrong side):** P 2, * sl 3 on dp needle, hold in back, k 3, k 3 from dp needle (back cable), sl 3 on dp needle, hold in front, k 3, k 3 from dp needle (front cable), p 2, repeat from * across. **Rows 2, 4, 6, 8, and 10:** K 2, * p 12, k 2, repeat from * across. **Rows 3, 5, 7, and 9:** P 2, * k 12, p 2, repeat from * across. **Row 11:** P 2, * back cable, front cable, p 2, repeat from * across. Repeat rows 2 through 11 for pattern.

[225]

Multiple of 16 sts plus 6: **Rows 1 and 3:** K 6, * p 1, k 8, p 1, k 6, repeat from * across. **Rows 2, 4, and 6:** P 6, * k 1, p 8, k 1, p 6, repeat from * across. **Row 5:** K 6, * p 1, sl 4 on dp needle, hold in back, k 4, k 4 from dp needle, p 1, k 6, repeat from * across.

[226]

Multiple of 12 sts plus 2: **Rows 1 and 3:** P 2, * k 1, p 2, k 4, p 2, k 1, p 2, repeat from * across. **Rows 2, 4, and 6:** K 2, * p 1, k 2, p 4, k 2, p 1, k 2, repeat from * across. **Row 5:** P 2, * k 1, p 2, sl 2 on dp needle, hold in back, k 2, k 2 from dp needle, p 2, k 1, p 2, repeat from * across.

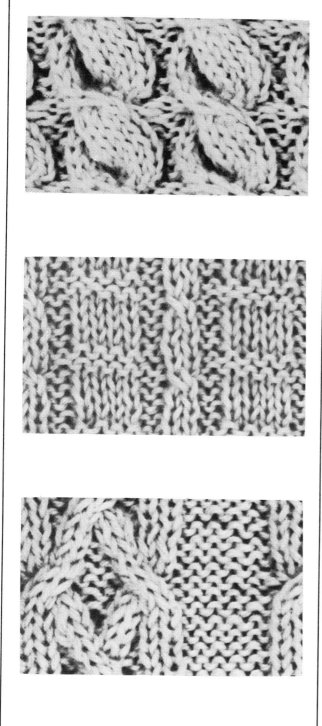

[227]

Multiple of 10 sts plus 2: **Rows 1, 3, and 7:** P 2, * k 8, p 2, repeat from * across. **Rows 2, 4, 6, and 8:** K 2, * p 8, k 2, repeat from * across. **Row 5:** P 2, * sl 6 on dp needle, hold in front, sk 1 st, insert right needle from left to right of back loop of next st, p this st, p the skipped st in same manner and drop both sts from left-hand needle, sl 2 from dp needle to left-hand needle, p these 2 sts through back loops, sl 3 from dp needle to left-hand needle, p these 3 sts through back loops, k 1 from dp needle drawing st up, p 2, repeat from * across.

[228]

Multiple of 10 sts: **Rows 1 and 3:** * K 2, p 2, k 2, p 2, k 2, repeat from * across. **Rows 2, 4, and 6:** K the p sts and p the k sts of previous row. **Row 5:** * P 4, sl 1 on dp needle, hold in front, k 1, k 1 from dp needle, p 4, repeat from * across.

[229]

Multiple of 18 sts: **Row 1:** P 3, * sl 2 on dp needle, hold in front, k 2, k 2 from dp needle (cable 4 front), p 4, sl 2 on dp needle, hold in back, k 2, k 2 from dp needle (cable 4 back), p 6, repeat from * across, and end p 3. **Rows 2 and 12:** K 3, * p 4, k 4, p 4, k 6, repeat from * across, and end k 3. **Row 3:** P 3, * k 2, sl 2 on dp needle, hold in front, p 1, k 2 from dp needle (cable 3 front), p 2, sl 1 on dp needle, hold in back, k 2, p 1 from dp needle (cable 3 back), k 2, p 6, repeat from * across, and end p 3. **Rows 4 and 10:** K 3, * p 2, k 1, p 2, k 2, p 2, k 1, p 2, k 6, repeat from * across, and end k 3. **Row 5:** P 3, * k 2, p 1, cable 3 front, cable 3 back, p 1, k 2, p 6, repeat from * across, and end p 3. **Rows 6 and 8:** K 3, * p 2, k 2, p 4, k 2, p 2, k 6, repeat from * across, and end k 3. **Row 7:** P 3, * k 2, p 2, cable 4 back, p 2, k 2, p 6, repeat from * across, and end p 3. **Row 9:** P 3, * k 2, p 1, cable 3 back, cable 3 front, p 1, k 2, p 6, repeat from * across, and end p 3. **Row 11:** P 3, * k 2, cable 3 back, p 2, cable 3 front, k 2, p 6, repeat from * across, and end p 3.

[230]
Multiple of 8 sts: **Row 1 (wrong side):** * K 4, p 4, repeat from * across. **Rows 2, 3, 4, and 6:** Repeat row 1. **Row 5:** * P 4, sl 2 on dp needle, hold in front, k 2, k 2 from dp needle, repeat from * across.

[231]
Multiple of 14 sts plus 4: **Rows 1, 3, and 5:** P 1, * k 2, p 3, k 6, p 3, repeat from * across, and end k 2, p 1. **Rows 2, 4, 6, and 8:** P. **Row 7:** P 1, * k 2, p 3, sl 3 on dp needle, hold in front, k 3, k 3 from dp needle, p 3, repeat from * across, and end k 2, p 1.

[232]
Multiple of 8 sts plus 2: **Rows 1, 3, and 11:** P 2, * k 6, p 2, repeat from * across. **Rows 2, 10, and 12:** K 2, * p 6, k 2, repeat from * across. **Rows 4, 6, and 8:** K 2, * p 2, sl 2 as if to p, p 2, k 2, repeat from * across. **Rows 5, 7, and 9:** P 2, * sl 2 on dp needle, hold in back, k 1, k 2 from dp needle, sl 1 on dp needle, hold in front, k 2, k 1 from dp needle, p 2, repeat from * across.

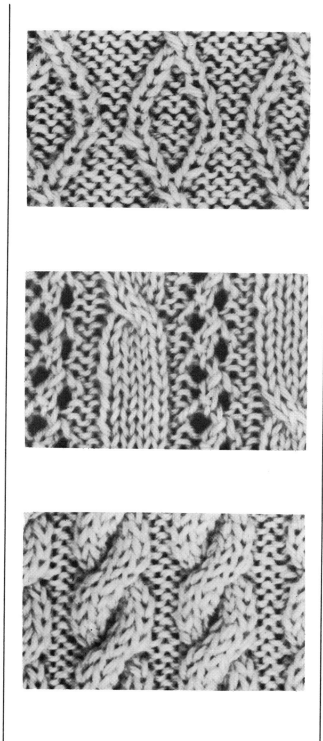

[233]

Multiple of 8 sts: **Row 1:** * P 1, k 1, p 4, k 1, p 1, repeat from * across. **Rows 2 and 12:** * K 1, p 1, k 4, p 1, k 1, repeat from * across. **Row 3:** * P 1, sl 1 on dp needle, hold in front, p 1, k 1 from dp needle (front twist), p 2, sl 1 on dp needle, hold in back, k 1, p 1 from dp needle (back twist), p 1, repeat from * across. **Rows 4 and 10:** * K 2, p 1, k 2, p 1, k 2, repeat from * across. **Row 5:** * P 2, front twist, back twist, p 2, repeat from * across. **Rows 6 and 8:** * K 3, p 2, k 3, repeat from * across. **Row 7:** * P 3, sl 1 on dp needle, hold in front, k 1, k 1 from dp needle, p 3, repeat from * across. **Row 9:** * P 2, back twist, front twist, p 2, repeat from * across. **Row 11:** * P 1, back twist, p 2, front twist, p 1, repeat from * across.

[234]

Multiple of 20 sts plus 8: **Rows 1, 5, 9, and 13:** * P 2, k 4, p 2, k 2 tog, yo, repeat from * across, and end p 2. **Rows 2, 4, 6, 8, 10, 12, 14, and 16:** * K 2, p 4, k 2, p 2, repeat from * across, and end k 2. **Rows 3 and 11:** * P 2, k 4, p 2, yo, sl 1 as if to p, k 1, psso, repeat from * across and end p 2. **Row 7:** * P 2, sl 2 on dp needle, hold in front, k 2, k 2 from dp needle, p 2, yo, sl 1 as if to p, k 1, psso, p 2, k 4, p 2, yo, sl 1 as if to p, k 1, psso, repeat from * across, and end p 2. **Row 15:** * P 2, k 4, p 2, yo, sl 1 as if to p, k 1, psso, p 2, sl 2 on dp needle, hold in front, k 2, k 2 from dp needle, p 2, yo, sl 1 as if to p, k 1, psso, repeat from * across, and end p 2.

[235]

Multiple of 9 sts plus 3: **Rows 1 and 3:** * P 3, k 6, repeat from * across, and end p 3. **Rows 2, 4, and 6:** * K 3, p 6, repeat from * across, and end k 3. **Row 5:** * P 3, sl 3 on dp needle, hold in back, k 3, k 3 from dp needle, repeat from * across, and end p 3.

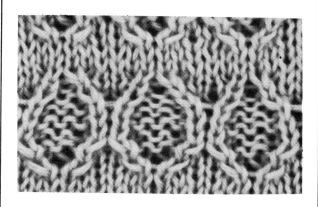

[236]
Multiple of 6 sts: **Row 1:** * P 2, k 2, p 2, repeat from * across. **Rows 2 and 12:** * K 2, p 2, k 2, repeat from * across. **Row 3:** * P 1, sl 1 on dp needle, hold in back, k 1, k 1 from dp needle, sl 1 on dp needle, hold in front, k 1, k 1 from dp needle, p 1, repeat from * across. **Rows 4 and 10:** * K 1, p 4, k 1, repeat from * across. **Row 5:** * Sl 1 on dp needle, hold in back, k 1, k 1 from dp needle, k 2, sl 1 on dp needle, hold in front, k 1, k 1 from dp needle, repeat from * across. **Rows 6 and 8:** P. **Row 7:** K. **Row 9:** * Sl 1 on dp needle, hold in front, k 1, k 1 from dp needle, k 2, sl 1 on dp needle, hold in back, k 1, k 1 from dp needle, repeat from * across. **Row 11:** * P 1, sl 1 on dp needle, hold in front, k 1, k 1 from dp needle, sl 1 on dp needle, hold in back, k 1, k 1 from dp needle, p 1, repeat from * across.

[237]
Multiple of 12 sts plus 4: **Rows 1, 3, and 5:** P 4, * k 2, p 4, repeat from * across. **Rows 2 and 4:** K 4, * p 2, k 4, repeat from * across. **Row 6:** K 4, * sl 2 as if to p, k 4, repeat from * across. **Row 7:** P 4, * sl 2 on dp needle, hold in front, p 2, yo, k 2 tog from dp needle, sl 2 on dp needle, hold in back, k 2 tog, yo, p 2 from dp needle, p 4, repeat from * across. **Row 8:** K 4, * p 2, k 1, p 2, k 1, p 2, k 4, repeat from * across.

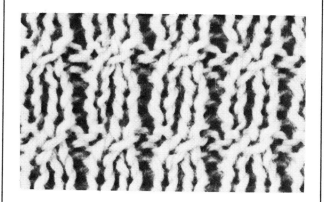

[238]
Multiple of 4 sts plus 1: **Rows 1 and 3:** * P 1, k 1, repeat from * across, and end p 1. **Rows 2, 4, and 6:** * K 1, p 1, repeat from * across, and end k 1. **Row 5:** * P 1, k the 3rd st on left-hand needle through front lp, p the 1st and 2nd sts and drop 3 sts from left-hand needle, repeat from * across, and end p 1.

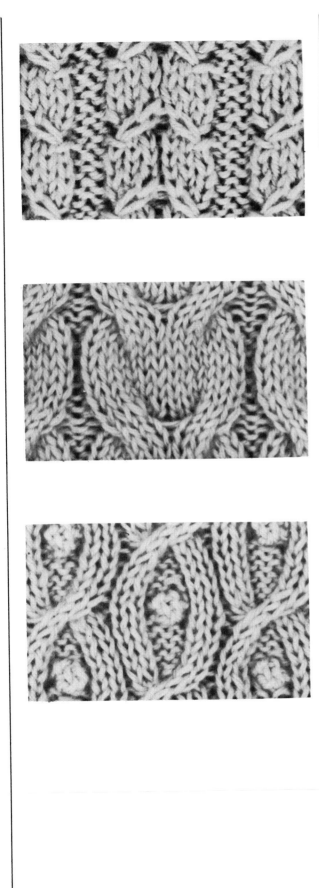

[239]

Multiple of 10 sts plus 3: **Row 1:** * P 3, k 3, p 1, k 3, repeat from * across, and end p 3. **Rows 2 and 6:** K 3, * p 3, k 1, p 3, k 3, repeat from * across. **Row 3:** * P 3, sl 1 as if to p, k 2, p 1, k 2, sl 1 as if to p, repeat from * across, and end p 3. **Row 4:** K 3, * sl 1 as if to p, p 2, k 1, p 2, sl 1 as if to p, k 3, repeat from * across. **Row 5:** * P 3, sl 1 on dp needle, hold in front, k 2, k 1 from dp needle, p 1, sl 2 on dp needle, hold in back, k 1, k 2 from dp needle, repeat from * across, and end p 3.

[240]

Multiple of 14 sts plus 2: **Row 1:** P 2, * sl 3 on dp needle, hold in back, k 3, k 3 from dp needle (back cable), sl 3 on dp needle, hold in front, k 3, k 3 from dp needle (front cable), p 2, repeat from * across. **Rows 2, 4, 6, 8, and 10:** K 2, * p 12, k 2, repeat from * across. **Rows 3, 5, 7, and 9:** P 2, * k 12, p 2, repeat from * across. **Row 11:** P 2, * back cable, front cable, p 2, repeat from * across. Repeat rows 2 through 11 for pattern.

[241]

Multiple of 32 sts: **Row 1:** * K 1, p 2, sl 6 on dp needle, hold in back, k 2, (p 4, k 2) from dp needle (8 st cable), p 1, k 2, p 1, (k 2, turn, p 2, turn) 3 times, (insert needle in 1st st on left-hand needle and in same st 6 rows below, k sts tog) twice (popcorn made), p 1, k 2, p 1, 8 st cable, p 2, k 1, repeat from * across. **Rows 2, 4, 6, 8, 10, and 12:** * P 1, k 2, (p 2, k 4, p 2, k 1) 3 times, k 1, p 1, repeat from * across. **Rows 3, 5, 9, and 11:** * K 1, p 2, (k 2, p 4, k 2, p 1) 3 times, p 1, k 1, repeat from * across. **Row 7:** * K 1, p 2, k 2, p 1, popcorn, p 1, k 2, p 1, 8 st cable, p 1, k 2, p 1, popcorn, p 1, k 2, p 2, k 1, repeat from * across.

[242]
Multiple of 18 sts: **Rows 1, 3, 5, 9, and 11:** K. **Rows 2, 4, 6, 8, 10, 12, and 14:** P. **Row 7:** * Sl 6 on dp needle, hold in front, k 6, k 6 from dp needle, repeat from * across, and end k 6. **Row 13:** * K 6, sl 6 on dp needle, hold in back, k 6, k 6 from dp needle, repeat from * across.

[243]
Multiple of 12 sts plus 4: **Rows 1, 3, 5, and 7:** * P 4, k 8, repeat from * across, and end p 4. **Rows 2, 4, 6, and 8:** * K 4, p 8, repeat from * across, and end k 4. **Row 9:** * P 4, sl 2 on dp needle, hold in back, k 2, k 2 from dp needle, sl 2 on dp needle, hold in front, k 2, k 2 from dp needle, repeat from * across, and end p 4. Repeat rows 2 through 9 for pattern.

[244]
Multiple of 7 sts plus 2: **Rows 1 and 5 (wrong side):** K 2, * p 5, k 2, repeat from * across. **Rows 2 and 6:** P 2, * k 2, sl 1 as if to k, k 2, p 2, repeat from * across. **Rows 3 and 7:** K 2, * p 2, sl 1 as if to p, p 2, k 2, repeat from * across. **Row 4:** P 2, * k 2, sl 1 on dp needle, hold in front, k 2, k 1 from dp needle, p 2, repeat from * across. **Row 8:** P 2, * k the 3rd st on left-hand needle through front lp, k the 1st and 2nd sts and drop 3 sts from left-hand needle, k 2, p 2, repeat from * across.

103

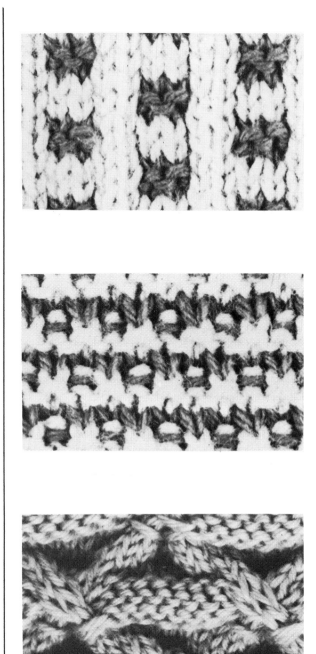

[245]
Multiple of 8 sts plus 4: **Row 1:** K 3 MC, * k 2 CC, k 6 MC, repeat from * across, and end k 1 CC. **Row 2:** K 1 CC, * p 6 MC, k 2 CC, repeat from * across, and end p 3 MC. **Row 3:** K 1 CC, * k 6 MC, k 2 CC, repeat from * across, and end k 3 MC. **Row 4:** P 3 MC, * k 2 CC, p 6 MC, repeat from * across, and end k 1 CC.

[246]
Multiple of 2 sts: **Rows 1, 2, 5, and 6:** With MC, k. **Rows 3 and 4:** With CC, * k 1, sl 1 as if to p, repeat from * across. **Rows 7 and 8:** With CC, * sl 1 as if to p, k 1, repeat from * across.

[247]
Multiple of 14 sts plus 7: **Row 1:** * P 7, sl 2, p 3, sl 2, repeat from * across, and end p 7. **Row 2:** * K 7, sl 2 on dp needle, hold in back, k 3, sl 2 as if to p from dp needle, sl 2, repeat from * across, and end k 7. **Row 3:** * P 7, sl 2 on dp needle, hold in front, sl 2 as if to k, p 3, sl 2 as if to k from dp needle, repeat from * across, and end p 7. **Row 4:** * K 7, p 2, k 3, p 2, repeat from * across, and end k 7. **Rows 5, 7, 9, 15, 17, and 19:** K. **Rows 6, 8, 10, 16, 18, and 20:** P. **Row 11:** * Sl 2, p 3, sl 2, p 7, repeat from * across, and end sl 2, p 3, sl 2. **Row 12:** * Sl 2 on dp needle, hold in back, k 3, sl 2 from dp needle, sl 2 (back cable), k 7, repeat from * across, and end back cable. **Row 13:** * Sl 2 as if to k on dp needle, hold in front, sl 2, p 3, sl 2 as if to k from dp needle (front cable), p 7, repeat from * across, and end front cable. **Row 14:** * P 2, k 3, p 2, k 7, repeat from * across, and end p 2, k 3, p 2.

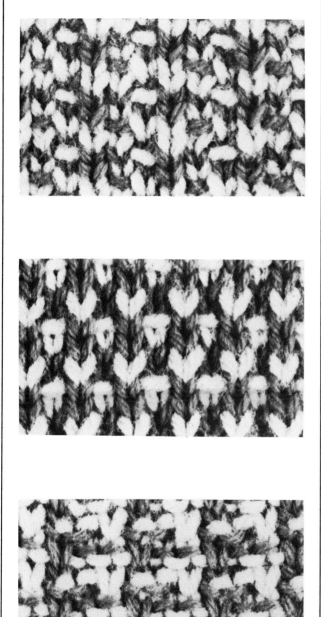

[248]
Multiple of 3 sts: **Row 1:** With MC, * sl 1 as if to p, k 2, repeat from * across. **Row 2:** With MC, p. **Row 3:** With CC, * k 2, sl 1 as if to p, repeat from * across. **Row 4:** With CC, p.

[249]
Multiple of 2 sts (work on dp needles): **Row 1 (wrong side):** With MC, p. Return to beg of row. **Row 2:** With CC, * p 1, sl 1, repeat from * across. **Row 3:** With MC, k. Return to beg of row. **Row 4:** With CC, * k 1, sl 1 as if to p, repeat from * across.

[250]
Multiple of 3 sts: **Row 1 (wrong side):** With CC, * sl 1 as if to p, k 2, repeat from * across. **Row 2:** With CC, k. **Row 3:** With MC, * k 2, sl 1 as if to p, repeat from * across. **Row 4:** With MC, k.

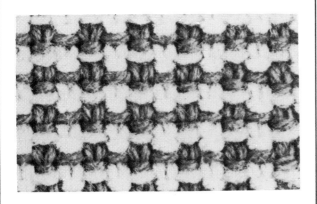

[251]
Multiple of 2 sts: **Row 1:** With MC, k 1, * k 1, sl 1 as if to p, repeat from * across, and end k 1. **Row 2:** With MC, k 1, * sl 1 as if to p, k 1, repeat from * across, and end k 2. **Row 3:** With CC, k 1, * sl 1 as if to p, k 1, repeat from * across, and end k 2. **Row 4:** With CC, k 1, * k 1, sl 1 as if to p, repeat from * across, and end k 1.

[252]
Multiple of 2 sts plus 1: **Row 1:** With CC, k. **Row 2:** With CC, p. **Row 3:** With MC, k 1, * sl 1 as if to p, k 1, repeat from * across. **Row 4:** With MC, * k 1, sl 1 as if to p, repeat from * across, and end k 1.

[253]
Multiple of 2 sts (work on dp needles): **Row 1:** With MC, * sl 1 as if to p, k 1, repeat from * across. **Row 2:** With CC, * sl 1, p 1, repeat from * across. Return to beg of row. **Row 3:** With MC, * p 1, k 1, repeat from * across. **Row 4:** With MC, * k 1, sl 1 as if to p, repeat from * across. Return to beg of row. **Row 5:** With CC, * sl 1 as if to p, k 1, repeat from * across. **Row 6:** With MC, * k 1, p 1, repeat from * across.

[254]

Multiple of 6 sts plus 5: **Row 1:** With CC, k 2, * sl 1 as if to p, k 5, repeat from * across, and end k 2. **Row 2:** With CC, p the k sts and sl the sl sts of previous row. **Rows 3 and 4:** With MC, * k 5, sl 1 as if to p, repeat from * across, and end k 5.

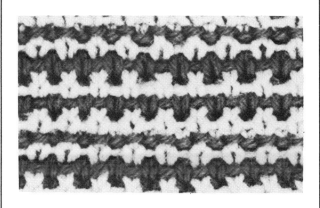

[255]

Multiple of 2 sts (work on dp needles): **Rows 1, 5, and 9:** With MC, * k 1, sl 1 as if to p, repeat from * across. Return to beg of row. **Rows 2, 6, 10, and 12:** With CC, * sl 1 as if to p, k 1, repeat from * across. **Rows 3 and 7:** With MC, p the MC sts and sl the CC sts of previous row. Return to beg of row. **Rows 4 and 8:** With CC, p the CC sts and sl the MC sts of previous row. **Row 11:** With MC, k the MC sts and sl the CC sts as if to p. Return to beg of row.

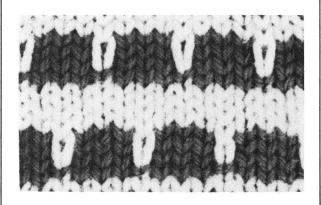

[256]

Multiple of 4 sts: **Row 1:** With CC, k. **Rows 2, 8, and 14:** With CC, p. **Rows 3 and 9:** With MC, k. **Rows 4 and 10:** With MC, p. **Rows 5 and 11:** With MC, k. **Rows 6 and 12:** With MC, p. **Row 7:** With CC, k 4, * with right-hand needle, draw up next CC st in row 2, yo, and pull through as a k st, drop off same st on left-hand needle, k 3, repeat from * across and end k 3. **Row 13:** With CC, k 2, * with right-hand needle draw up next CC st in row 7, yo and pull through as a k st, drop off same st on left-hand needle, k 3, repeat from * across, and end k 1.

[257]
Multiple of 6 sts plus 3: **Row 1:** K 4 MC, * k 1 CC, k 5 MC, repeat from * across, and end k 4 MC. **Row 2:** * P 3 MC, p 1 CC, p 1 MC, p 1 CC, repeat from * across, and end p 3 MC. **Rows 3 and 5:** With MC, k. **Rows 4 and 6:** With MC, p.

[258]
Multiple of 4 sts: **Row 1:** * K 2 MC, k 2 CC, repeat from * across. **Row 2:** * P 2 CC, p 2 MC, repeat from * across. **Row 3:** * K 2 CC, k 2 MC, repeat from * across. **Row 4:** * P 2 MC, p 2 CC, repeat from * across.

[259]
Multiple of 4 sts: **Rows 1, 2, 5, 6, 9, 10, 13, and 14:** With MC, k. **Row 3:** With CC, * k 3, sl 1 as if to p, repeat from * across. **Rows 4, 8, 12, and 16:** With CC, p CC sts and sl MC sts of previous row. **Row 7:** With CC, k 2, * sl 1 as if to p, k 3, repeat from * across, and end k 1. **Row 11:** With CC, k 1, * sl 1 as if to p, k 3, repeat from * across, and end sl 1, k 2. **Row 15:** With CC, * sl 1 as if to p, k 3, repeat from * across.

[260]
Multiple of 8 sts plus 7: **Row 1:** K 3 CC, * k 1 MC, k 7 CC, repeat from * across, and end k 1 MC, k 3 CC. **Rows 2, 4, 6, 8, 10, 12, 14, and 16:** Working color over color, p. **Rows 3 and 15:** K 2 CC, * k 3 MC, k 5 CC, repeat from * across, and end k 3 MC, k 2 CC. **Rows 5 and 13:** K 1 CC, * k 5 MC, k 3 CC, repeat from * across, and end k 5 MC, k 1 CC. **Rows 7 and 11:** * K 7 MC, k 1 CC, repeat from * across, and end k 7 MC. **Row 9:** With MC, k.

[261]
Multiple of 6 sts plus 3: **Rows 1 and 3:** K 3 MC, * k 1 CC, k 5 MC, repeat from * across. **Row 2:** P 1 CC, * p 3 MC, p 3 CC, repeat from * across, and end p 2 MC. **Rows 4 and 6:** P 2 MC, * p 1 CC, p 5 MC, repeat from * across, and end p 1 CC. **Row 5:** K 2 CC, * k 3 MC, k 3 CC, repeat from * across, and end k 1 MC.

[262]
Multiple of 7 sts: **Rows 1 and 3:** K 3 MC, * k 1 CC, k 6 MC, repeat from * across, and end k 1 CC, k 3 MC. **Rows 2 and 10:** Working color over color, p. **Row 4:** P 4 MC, * p 1 CC, p 6 MC, repeat from * across, and end p 1 CC, p 2 MC. **Row 5:** Working color over color, k. **Row 6:** * P 5 CC, p 2 MC, repeat from * across. **Row 7:** * K 1 CC, k 1 MC, k 3 CC, k 2 MC, repeat from * across. **Row 8:** P 2 MC, * p 4 CC, p 3 MC, repeat from * across, and end p 4 CC, p 1 MC. **Row 9:** K 4 MC, * k 1 CC, k 6 MC, repeat from * across, and end k 1 CC, k 2 MC.

[263]
Multiple of 2 sts: **Row 1:** With CC, p. **Row 2:** With MC, * k 1, sl 1 as if to p, repeat from * across. **Row 3:** With MC, p. **Row 4:** With CC, k 1, * k 1, sl 1 as if to p, repeat from * across, and end k 1.

[264]
Multiple of 4 sts: **Row 1:** K 2 CC, * k 1 MC, k 3 CC, repeat from * across, and end k 1 CC. **Row 2:** * P 1 CC, p 3 MC, repeat from * across. **Row 3:** * K 1 CC, k 3 MC, repeat from * across. **Row 4:** P 2 CC, * p 1 MC, p 3 CC, repeat from * across, and end p 1 CC.

[265]
Multiple of 6 sts: **Row 1:** With MC, * p 2, turn, k 2, turn, p 3, turn, k 3, turn, p 4, turn, k 4, turn, p 5, turn, k 5, turn, p 6, turn, k 6, turn, p 6, repeat from * across. **Row 2:** With CC, inc 1 st in 1st st, sl 1, k 1, psso, turn, p 3, turn, inc 1 in 1st st, k 1, sl 1, k 1, psso, turn, p 4, turn, inc 1 in 1st st, k 2 sl 1, k 1, psso, turn, p 5, turn, inc 1 in 1st st, k 3, sl 1, k 1, psso, * with same needle pick up and k 6 down side of MC triangle, turn, p 6, turn. ** K 5, k the 6th st tog with 1st st of next MC triangle, turn, p 6, turn, repeat from ** until all 6 sts of MC triangle are worked, then repeat from * across. Before turning for 3rd row, pick up and k 6 sts on outside edge of last MC triangle, turn, p 2 tog, p 4, turn, k 5, turn, p 2 tog, p 3, turn, k 4, turn, p 2 tog, p 2, turn, k 3, turn, p 2 tog, p 1, turn, k 2, turn, p 2 tog, turn, k 1. Break off CC. **Row 3:** With MC, p 1, pick up and p 5 sts down side of last CC triangle, * turn, ** k 6, turn, p 5, p 6th st tog with next CC st, turn, repeat from ** until all CC sts are worked off. Pick up and p 6 sts at side of CC triangle and repeat from * across. Repeat rows 2 and 3 for pattern. To bind off, on row 2 when 4 CC sts remain, bind off 1 st at beg of each k row.

[266]
Multiple of 8 sts plus 1: **Row 1:** * K 1 MC, k 7 CC, repeat from * across, and end k 1 MC. **Rows 2 and 6:** * P 2 MC, p 5 CC, p 1 MC, repeat from * across, and end p 2 MC. **Rows 3, 5, 7, 11, 13, and 15:** Working color over color, k. **Row 4:** * P 3 MC, p 3 CC, p 2 MC, repeat from * across, and end p 3 MC. **Row 8:** P 1 MC, * p 7 CC, p 1 MC, repeat from * across. **Row 9:** * K 4 CC, k 1 MC, k 3 CC, repeat from * across, and end k 4 CC. **Rows 10 and 14:** * P 3 CC, p 3 MC, p 2 CC, repeat from * across, and end p 3 CC. **Row 12:** * P 2 CC, p 5 MC, p 1 CC, repeat from * across, and end p 2 CC. **Row 16:** * P 4 CC, p 1 MC, p 3 CC, repeat from * across, and end p 4 CC.

[267]
Multiple of 6 sts plus 2: **Row 1:** K 2 MC, * k 4 CC, k 2 MC, repeat from * across. **Row 2:** * P 2 MC, p 4 CC, repeat from * across, and end p 2 MC. **Rows 3 and 7:** K 2 CC, * (k 1 MC, k 2 CC) twice, repeat from * across. **Rows 4 and 8:** With CC, p. **Row 5:** K 3 CC, * k 2 MC, k 4 CC, repeat from * across, and end k 3 CC. **Row 6:** * P 3 CC, p 2 MC, p 1 CC, repeat from * across, and end p 3 CC.

[268]
Multiple of 9 sts: **Rows 1, 9, and 17:** * K 4 MC, k 3 CC, k 2 MC, repeat from * across. **Rows 2, 8, 10, 16, 18, and 24:** * P 2 MC, p 2 CC, p 5 MC, repeat from * across. **Rows 3 and 11:** * K 5 MC, k 1 CC, k 3 MC, repeat from * across. **Rows 4, 6, 12, 14, 20, and 22:** * P 1 MC, p 2 CC, p 6 MC, repeat from * across. **Rows 5, 13, and 21:** * K 6 MC, k 3 CC, repeat from * across. **Row 7:** * K 6 MC, k 2 CC, k 1 MC, repeat from * across. **Rows 15 and 23:** * K 7 MC, k 1 CC, k 1 MC, repeat from * across. **Row 19:** * K 5 MC, k 2 CC, k 2 MC, repeat from * across.

[269]

Multiple of 9 sts plus 8: **Row 1:** * K 1 MC, k 6 CC, k 2 MC, repeat from * across, and end k 1 MC. **Row 2:** * P 2 CC, p 4 MC, p 2 CC, p 1 MC, repeat from * across, and end p 2 CC. **Row 3:** * K 1 CC, k 2 MC, k 2 CC, k 2 MC, k 2 CC, repeat from * across, and end k 1 CC. **Row 4:** * P 1 CC, p 2 MC, p 2 CC, p 2 MC, p 2 CC, repeat from * across, and end p 1 CC. **Row 5:** * K 2 CC, k 4 MC, k 2 CC, k 1 MC, repeat from * across, and end k 2 CC. **Row 6:** * P 1 MC, p 6 CC, p 2 MC, repeat from * across, and end p 1 MC. **Row 7:** With MC, k. **Row 8:** With MC, p.

[270]

Multiple of 4 sts plus 1: **Row 1:** With CC, k. **Row 2:** * P 1 MC, p 3 CC, repeat from * across, and end p 1 MC. **Row 3:** * K 1 CC, k 1 MC, repeat from * across, and end k 1 CC. **Row 4:** * P 2 CC, p 1 MC, p 1 CC, repeat from * across, and end p 2 CC.

[271]

Multiple of 4 sts plus 1: **Rows 1, 2, 5, and 6:** With A, k. **Row 3:** K 1 C, * k 1 B, k 1 C, repeat from * across. **Row 4:** P 1 C, * p 3 B, p 1 C, repeat from * across. **Row 7:** K 2 C, * k 1 B, k 3 C, repeat from * across, and end k 2 C. **Row 8:** P 2 C, * p 1 B, p 3 C, repeat from * across, and end p 2 C.

[272]
Multiple of 4 sts: **Rows 1 and 7 (wrong side):** With A, p. **Row 2:** * K 1 B, k 3 A, repeat from * across. **Row 3:** P 1 B, * p 1 A, p 3 B, repeat from * across, and end p 2 B. **Row 4:** With B, k. **Row 5:** * P 3 B, p 1 A, repeat from * across. **Row 6:** K 2 A, * k 1 B, k 3 A, repeat from * across, and end k 1 A. **Row 8:** * K 1 C, k 3 A, repeat from * across. **Row 9:** P 1 C, * p 1 A, p 3 C, repeat from * across, and end p 2 C. **Row 10:** With C, k. **Row 11:** * P 3 C, p 1 A, repeat from * across. **Row 12:** K 2 A, * k 1 C, k 3 A, repeat from * across, and end k 1 A.

[273]
Multiple of 2 sts: **Row 1:** With B, * k 1, sl 1 as if to p, repeat from * across. **Row 2:** With C, * p 1, sl 1 as if to k, repeat from * across. Repeat rows 1 and 2 for pattern, alternating colors A, B, and C on every row.

[274]
Multiple of 6 sts plus 3: **Rows 1 and 3:** With A, k. **Rows 2 and 4:** P 3 A, * p 3 B, p 3 A, repeat from * across. **Rows 5 and 7:** * K 3 C, k 3 A, repeat from * across, and end k 3 C. **Rows 6 and 8:** P 3 C, * p 3 A, p 3 C, repeat from * across. **Rows 9 and 10:** With A, k.

[275]

Multiple of 10 sts plus 9: **Rows 1 and 3:** With A, k. **Row 2:** * P 2 A, p 2 B, repeat from * across, and end p 1 B. **Rows 4 and 12:** With B, p. **Rows 5 and 11:** K 1 B, * k 2 B, k 3 C, k 5 B, repeat from * across, and end k 3 B. **Rows 6 and 10:** * P 2 B, p 2 C, p 1 B, p 2 C, p 3 B, repeat from * across, and end p 2 B. **Rows 7 and 9:** * K 1 B, k 2 C, k 3 B, k 2 C, k 2 B, repeat from * across, and end k 1 B. **Row 8:** * P 2 C, p 2 B, p 1 A, p 2 B, p 2 C, p 1 B, repeat from * across, and end p 2 C.

[276]

Multiple of 18 sts plus 1: **Row 1:** With A, k. **Row 2:** With B, p. **Row 3:** * K 1 C, k 2 B, k 4 A, k 2 B, k 4 C, k 2 B, k 3 C, repeat from * across, and end k 4 C. **Rows 4 and 6:** * (P 1 C, p 2 B) 4 times, p 4 A, p 2 B, repeat from * across, and end p 1 C. **Row 5:** * K 1 C, k 2 B, k 4 A, (k 2 B, k 1 C) 3 times, k 2 B, repeat from * across, and end k 1 C. **Row 7:** * K 1 C, k 8 B, k 1 C, k 2 B, k 4 C, k 2 B, repeat from * across, and end k 1 C. **Row 8:** * P 1 C, p 8 B, p 1 C, p 2 B, p 4 C, p 2 B, repeat from * across, and end p 1 C. **Row 9:** * (K 1 C, k 2 B) 4 times, k 4 A, k 2 B, repeat from * across, and end k 1 C. **Rows 10 and 12:** * P 1 C, p 2 B, p 4 A, p 2 B, (p 1 C, p 2 B) 3 times, repeat from * across, and end p 1 C. **Row 11:** * (K 1 C, k 2 B) 4 times, K 4 A, k 2 B, repeat from * across, and end k 1 C. **Row 13:** With B, k. **Row 14:** With A, p.

[277]

Multiple of 16 sts plus 14: **Row 1:** * K 2 A, k 2 B, k 12 A, repeat from * across, and end k 10 A. **Rows 2, 4, 6, 8, 10, 12, and 14:** Working color over color, p. **Row 3:** * K 2 B, k 2 C, k 2 B, k 4 A, k 2 B, k 4 A, repeat from * across, and end k 2 A. **Row 5:** * K 2 C, k 2 B, k 2 C, k 4 B, k 2 C, k 4 B, repeat from * across, and end k 2 B. **Row 7:** * K 6 C, k 2 B, repeat from * across, and end k 6 C. **Row 9:** * K 2 B, k 2 C, k 4 B, k 2 C, k 2 B, k 2 C, k 2 B, repeat from * across, and end k 2 C. **Row 11:** * K 2 A, k 2 B, k 4 A, k 2 B, k 2 C, k 2 B, k 2 A, repeat from * across, and end k 2 B. **Row 13:** * K 10 A, k 2 B, k 4 A, repeat from * across, and end k 2 A.

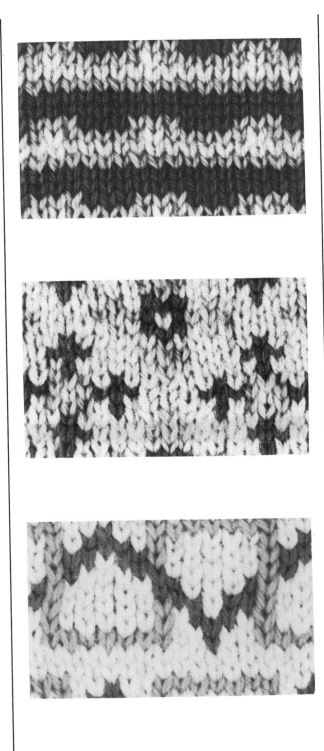

[278]
Multiple of 6 sts plus 1: **Row 1:** With A, k. **Row 2:** * P 1 A, p 5 B, repeat from * across, and end p 1 A. **Row 3:** * K 2 B, k 3 C, k 1 B, repeat from * across, and end k 2 B. **Row 4:** With C, p. **Row 5:** With C, k. **Row 6:** With B, p.

[279]
Multiple of 12 sts plus 7: **Rows 1 and 11:** * K 2 C, k 1 A, k 1 B, k 5 A, k 1 B, k 1 A, k 1 C, repeat from * across, and end k 3 A. **Rows 2, 4, 8, and 10:** * P 1 C, p 5 A, p 1 B, p 5 A, repeat from * across, and end p 1 B. **Rows 3 and 9:** * K 2 B, k 3 A, k 3 C, k 3 A, k 1 B, repeat from * across, and end k 2 C. **Rows 5 and 7:** * K 3 A, k 1 C, k 1 A, k 3 B, k 1 A, k 1 C, k 2 A, repeat from * across, and end k 2 B. **Row 6:** * P 1 A, p 1 B, p 3 C, p 3 A, p 3 C, p 1 B, repeat from * across, and end p 2 A. **Row 12:** * P 2 A, p 3 B, p 1 C, p 1 A, p 1 C, p 3 B, p 1 A, repeat from * across, and end p 1 A.

[280]
Multiple of 12 sts plus 1: **Row 1:** With A, k. **Row 2:** * P 1 B, p 2 A, p 1 C, p 2 A, p 6 B, repeat from * across, and end p 7 B. **Row 3:** * K 1 B, k 5 A, k 1 B, k 1 A, k 3 C, k 1 A, repeat from * across, and end k 1 B. **Row 4:** * P 1 B, p 2 C, p 1 A, p 2 C, p 1 B, p 5 A, repeat from * across, and end p 1 B. **Row 5:** * K 1 C, k 5 A, k 1 B, k 1 C, k 3 A, k 1 C, repeat from * across, and end k 2 C. **Row 6:** * P 1 C, p 5 A, p 1 B, p 1 C, p 3 A, p 1 C, repeat from * across, and end p 2 C. **Row 7:** * K 1 B, k 2 C, k 1 A, k 2 C, k 1 B, k 5 A, repeat from * across, and end k 1 B. **Row 8:** * P 1 B, p 5 A, p 1 B, p 1 A, p 3 C, p 1 A, repeat from * across, and end p 1 B. **Row 9:** * K 1 B, k 2 A, k 1 C, k 2 A, k 6 B, repeat from * across, and end k 7 B. **Row 10:** With A, p.

Alphabet charts

Appearing below are two alphabet charts, the letters of which are often used for the knitting in of a name or monogram as part of the design of a sweater. The stitch usually used to do this is the stockinette stitch (knit 1 row, purl 1 row), and each box on the alphabet chart represents one stitch horizontally and one row vertically.

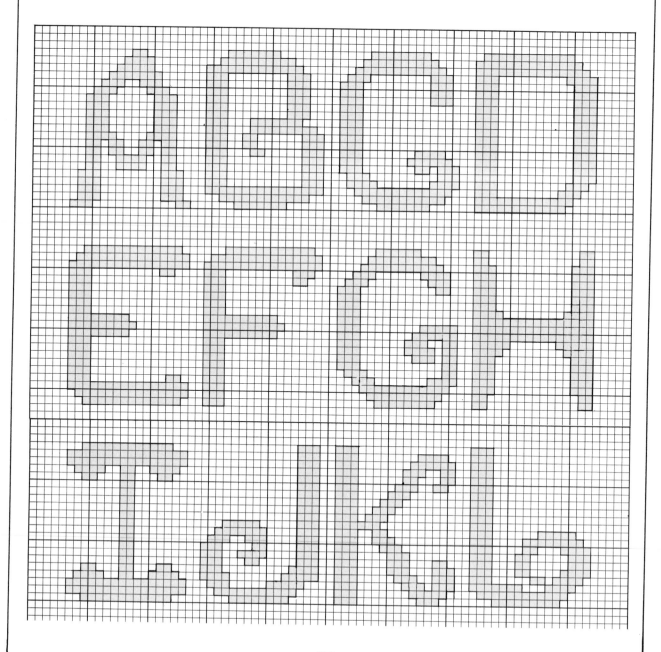

MNOP
QRST
UVWX
YZ

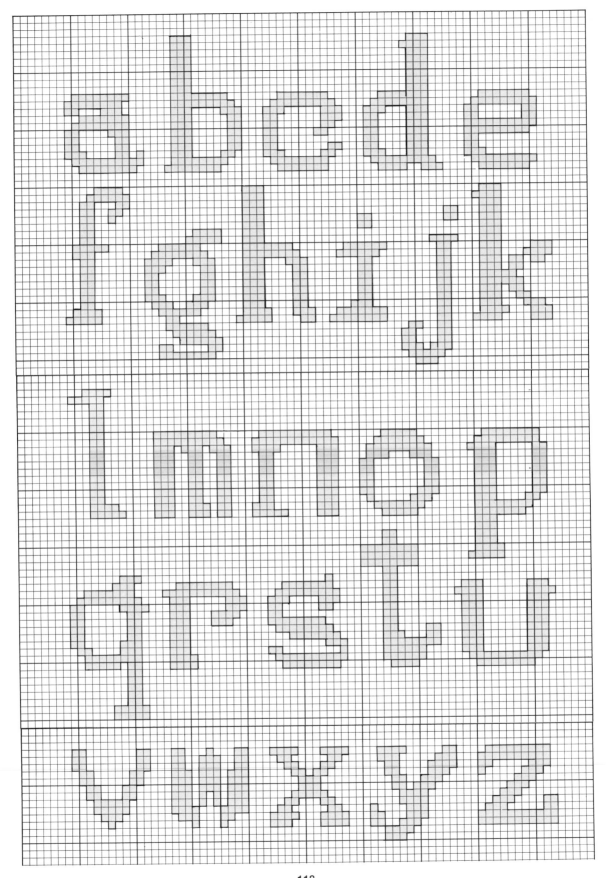

7

Knitter's guide

In order to be a knitter you need to know only three basic techniques: how to "cast on," or get starting stitches onto a needle; how to "knit," or by inserting the second of your pair of needles into each stitch on your first needle, putting the yarn over the second needle and drawing it through, you continue to make more stitches, and you are already knitting; and how to "bind off," or remove all stitches from both needles and finish off when your work is done. Illustrations for these three techniques are given below. Try them, practice them on a few stitches for a while, and when you feel that the needles and yarn are comfortable in your hands, and that you have mastered what you are doing, you are a knitter, and able to make a large straight piece of any size, such as a scarf or a rug, in garter stitch, which is an all "knit" stitch.

Having come this far, however, you will be wanting to know other things, such as, almost immediately, how many stitches you will need to cast on in order to make your piece the width you want it to be. This we will explain to you in a paragraph on "gauge," which follows here shortly and tells you how to measure and calculate the number of stitches for the exact size you want. After this, you will also want to know how to "purl," for most stitches, aside from the all-knit garter stitch you

have just mastered, involve the use of the "purl" stitch, including the basic stockinette stitch, which is the one used more than any other in knitting and is worked by alternating 1 row knit and 1 row purl. As one thing leads to another, you will want to learn about many more things to do with your knitting, including how to increase and decrease and how to pick up stitches, make cables and buttonholes, work a "yarn over" to achieve a lacy effect, work with more than one color of yarn, embroider a duplicate stitch, form a hemline, pick up a dropped stitch, and so on until you know everything there is to know about the craft. With a little patience and practice, you will soon know all these things and be able to make anything you want, and make it well.

Gauge

Gauge, in knitting, means the number of stitches you are getting to an inch with your two needles, your ball of yarn, and the pattern stitch you are working with. It is an important word to know, perhaps one of the most important in knitting, because without it you cannot possibly calculate the number of stitches you need, or achieve a proper fit or size. The number of stitches you get to each inch of your work, multiplied by the number of inches you want your work to measure, determines the number of stitches you need to work with; without this information, you cannot even begin. The yarn you are using, the needles and the pattern stitch and the tension of your own two hands, are what determine the gauge you are getting. Most yarn labels suggest a stitch and row gauge and the size needles you would use to get them. Since personal tension, however, is a complete variable, some may get the suggested gauge on the suggested needles, while others may need to use needles as different as three sizes larger or smaller from those suggested. Also, if you are designing your own knits, you just might be wanting to achieve a "feel" either very much looser or tighter than the one suggested on the label of the yarn you have chosen.

There is a definite procedure to follow in determining your gauge, and that is to work a small piece, about 3 inches square, in the pattern stitch you are using and with the yarn you have selected and the suggested needles. You will see directly how many stitches you are getting to the inch. If you are working from a pattern and it calls, for example, for 5 stitches to an inch and you are getting 7, you must change to larger needles, experimenting with a few sizes until you find the ones that give you the 5. If you are getting 3 stitches instead of 5, then you must switch to smaller needles until you find the right ones. In designs of your own, you experiment in exactly the same way until you reach your own desired gauge.

In many garments the row gauge does not matter too much, as long as you have gotten the proper number of stitches to the inch, but in others, such as one involving, for example, a raglan shaping, it is very important. An average tension generally works out best with a certain number of rows per inch, this in proportion to the number of stitches you are getting, presuming you are working with an average pattern stitch and not one involving an elongated stitch of any type. A simple stockinette stitch with 3 stitches to an inch generally, at best gauge, has 5 rows to an inch, as 4 stitches have 6 rows, 5 stitches 7 rows, and so on. If you are striving for one of these specific gauges, and you find you are getting, for example, 3 stitches and only 4 rows, instead of the suggested 5 rows, on No. 10 needles, you might try No. 11 needles, on which you will probably get the same 3 stitches, yet obtain the necessary 5 rows.

In any case, having reached your desired gauge you would then multiply the width of whatever it is you are making by the number of stitches you are getting to an inch, and you would know immediately how many stitches you will need to cast on. For in-

stance, a 10-inch-wide scarf at a 3 stitch to 1 inch gauge would be worked on 30 stitches; on a 5 stitch to 1 inch gauge, it would be worked on 50 stitches; and on a 7 stitch to 1 inch gauge, it would be worked on 70 stitches. In the making of this particular scarf, the number of rows you get to an inch does not matter, and you would just work for a certain number of inches until you have reached the desired length. On the other hand, in the shaping, for example, of a raglan sleeve, you would need to observe your row gauge and then, in the process of shaping, calculate the number of rows you are getting to, let us say, a presumed 8-inch armhole shaping, multiply the 8 inches by your row gauge, and divide the total number of rows by the number of stitches you must "lose," or decrease, for your shaping in that number of rows in as gradual a way as possible. If on a presumed gauge of 7 rows to 1 inch, that armhole you want would involve 56 rows, and if the number of stitches you have on your needle were 50, and you were decreasing 1 stitch at each end of your needle, you would need to figure the disposition of 50 stitches in the 56 rows. Or, actually, since you are decreasing 2 stitches on each row, 25 decreases in 56 rows, you would now seek the closest multiple of 25 to 56 and, finding that it is 2, you would know that, by decreasing 1 stitch at either end of your needles on every other row, you would have worked your decreases within 50 rows, and remain with 6 stitches left over. Since, however, you want to work through all of the 56 rows instead of just 50 and remain with no stitches on your needles, you would calculate again and probably come to shape your piece by decreasing 1 stitch at each end of your needle every 4th row 3 times, then every other row 22 times, thus decreasing your 50 stitches in 56 rows and having worked out a well-shaped raglan armhole.

Whether your knitting of the moment involves both your stitch and row gauge or your stitch gauge only, remember that it is of utmost importance for you to test first with your yarn and needles before attempting any project, swatching and sampling it out for a few inches to make sure that it maintains itself at an even level and is comfortable to work. Having done this much, you can be sure that what you are making will be the proper size and that it will fit right.

Note: All technique illustrations and directions appearing below represent the knitting methods we prefer, and they have been used in the making of all pattern stitches appearing in this book. Should there be a variation in your own particular method of knitting, such as inserting your right needle into the next stitch on your left needle through the back rather than through the front as we do, then there may be a slight variation in the appearance of some of your stitches.

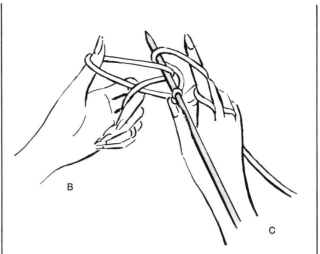

through loop and pull short and down to tighten it (**D**). (4) Repeat from * for desired number of stitches.

Casting on

Make a loop on needle, allowing a 2-yard end of yarn for every 100 stitches that need to be cast on, more if your yarn is a heavier than average weight, and less if it is lighter. This is your first stitch (**A**).

Hold needle in your right hand with short end of yarn toward you, then * (1) with short end make a loop on left thumb and insert needle from front to back through this loop (**B**), (2) place yarn attached to ball under and around needle (**C**), (3) draw yarn

Knitting

Holding needle with cast-on stitches in your left hand with yarn to back of work, * insert right needle from left to right through front of first stitch, wrap yarn completely around right needle forming a loop, slip needle and loop through stitch to front, and slip stitch just worked off left needle. This is your first knit stitch. Repeat from * in same manner across all stitches on left needle.

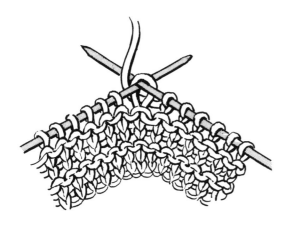

Binding off

Knit first 2 stitches, then * insert point of left needle into the 1st stitch on right needle (**A**) and lift this

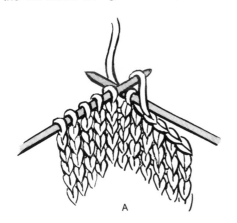

stitch over the 2nd stitch and drop off needle (**B**). Knit another stitch and repeat from * across for necessary number of stitches to be bound off. When all stitches are to be bound off at the end of a piece of work, and when one stitch remains,

break off yarn and fasten off by drawing remaining yarn through that last stitch.

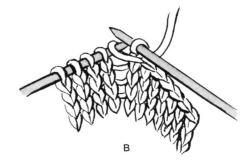

Purling

* Holding yarn in front of work, insert right needle from right to left through front of first stitch on left needle, wrap yarn completely around right needle, forming a loop, slip needle and loop through stitch to back, and slip stitch just worked off left needle. Repeat from * until all stitches are worked.

Increasing

Insert right needle from right to left through back of next stitch on left needle, wrap yarn completely around needle, forming a loop (**A**), and slip needle and loop through to front, forming a new stitch on right needle, then knit the same stitch on left needle in usual manner (**B**), and slip the stitch from left needle.

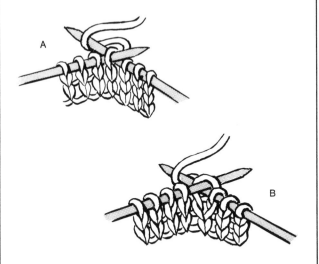

Decreasing

Insert right needle through 2 stitches on left needle and work these stitches together as one stitch.

Picking up stitches

Picking up stitches, as is necessary around a neck or an armhole, is always done on the right side of work, and one usually starts at a seam edge, such as the top of one shoulder for neck stitches, or at the underarm for an armhole shaping. Stitches are picked up by inserting your right needle through center of desired stitch and knitting that stitch in usual manner onto right needle, fitting the number of stitches evenly into the complete space available for the picking up of your stitches.

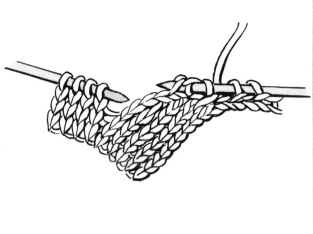

Picking up dropped stitches

Unintentionally dropped stitches are most often picked up on the right side of work, and with the use of a crochet hook. To pick up a dropped stitch, insert a crochet hook into the dropped stitch, * catch the loose strand of yarn of the next row in back of the hook and pull the loop through on hook. Repeat from * up each strand of yarn until the top strand has been pulled through, then place the last loop on left needle and continue with your knitting.

type of twist involved in the pattern stitch, and then knitted after the necessary number of stitches have been worked from the left needle.

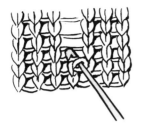

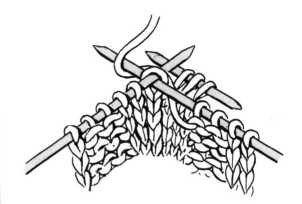

Yarn over

When knitting, wrap yarn under and around right needle as shown, forming a loop. When purling, wrap yarn over and around right needle, then work next stitch in either case as indicated in pattern being worked, thus adding a simulated stitch to form an eyelet hole.

Forming buttonholes

To form buttonholes, work to within the number of stitches at which point your buttonholes will occur, then bind off as many stitches as are necessary to accommodate the size of the button being used (A) and complete row. On the next row, cast on 1 stitch over each stitch bound off on previous row (B). Buttonholes are usually finished for firmness by sewing an overcast stitch around each one when the garment is completed.

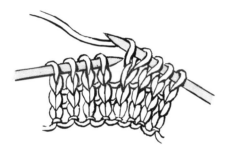

Cables

Cables are worked as they read in pattern instructions. A double-point needle is always used as the cable needle, and stitches are slipped on it and held in front or back of the work, depending on the

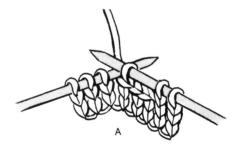

A

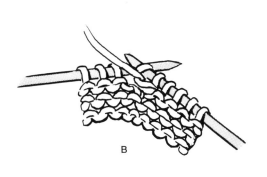

B

Multicolored knitting

When changing colors along the row, always bring the new color to be used from under and around the color just dropped so that the yarn is twisted in back and the work lies flat and smooth. The color not being used must always be carried loosely across the back so that it does not "draw together" the stitches being worked. When a second color is carried for more than 5 or 6 stitches, it should be twisted in back with the first color about midway to secure the second color in place, and to avoid having long loose-hanging threads on the wrong side of work. When a change of color occurs after a span of more than 8 stitches, a separate strand of yarn should be used.

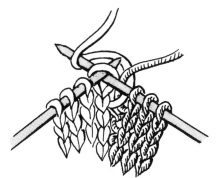

Slip stitch

Insert right needle from right to left through front of stitch to be slipped and transfer it onto right needle, without changing position of yarn. To slip stitch as if to knit when the previous stitch is a purl stitch, bring yarn to back of work before transferring. To slip stitch as if to purl when the previous stitch is a knit stitch, bring yarn to front of work.

Pass slip stitch over

To pass slip stitch over means to lift the slipped stitch with the point of the left needle, pass it over the next one or two stitches, as specified, and drop it from left needle.

Ribbing

Ribbing is a combination of knit and purl stitches, and it may be worked in any multiple depending on the width of the rib desired. Popular ribs are the narrow knit 1, purl 1; the wider knit 2, purl 2; the still wider knit 3, purl 3; or any variation of these, such as knit 2, purl 1, knit 3, purl 2, and so on. In all ribbed stitches, always knit the purl stitches and purl the knit stitches of previous row. Ribbing is used generally to shape parts of a garment where a "drawing-in" holding effect is desired, such as at the bottom of a sweater or around the neckband or for a slim waistband shaping, and is quite often worked, for this reason, on needles two or three sizes smaller than that used for the rest of the garment.

Four-needle knitting

Four double-point needles are often used for knitting small seamless items, such as socks or mittens. Casting on for this type of knitting is done in the same manner as for straight needles, except that the number of stitches to be cast on is evenly divided onto three needles and the fourth one is a free one to be used for knitting. As the stitches from the first needle are transferred onto the free needle, that first needle becomes the free one and is used for knitting into the next group of stitches. In this type of knitting, needles should be held firmly and the yarn held taut in transferring from one needle to another so that no open spaces occur. Since this is knitting "in the round," you need to be careful that stitches are not twisted. Because with four needles all the knitting is done on the right side of work, a stitch such as stockinette, which involves 1 row knit and 1 row purl on straight needles, would be worked in all knit on the four needles.

Round needle knitting

Round needle knitting, similar to that done on four needles, is a circular form of knitting, where no seaming is desired. A round needle is very flexible, except for the points, and can accommodate a large number of stitches. Casting on is done as for any other type of knitting, and on the first round of knitting, after casting on, you need to be sure that the yarn is pulled quite taut for the first stitch, and that the work is held straight and the stitches are not twisted. Again, as for four-needle knitting, all the work is done on the right side and, as in the stockinette stitch, where the first row is knitted and the second purled on straight needles (the purl side being the wrong side), so with a round needle all stitches are knitted. There are instances when, where a very large number of stitches are involved, a round needle is used because of its flexibility for back-and-forth straight knitting. When this is desired, the work is not joined at the end of the first round, but rather, one turns the needle and works each row back and forth in the usual manner.

Seaming

There are three popular methods of seaming and putting pieces together. One is a woven seam, one a sewn seam, and one a crocheted seam. In all three, the pieces to be joined must be matched carefully, and the seaming is done with the same yarn as that with which the pieces were worked. In the last two instances, a ¼-inch allowance on each side of each part of the garment needs to be made because this is approximately the amount that will be taken up in the seaming process. Woven seams are worked with a blunt-edge tapestry needle. Starting at an upper edge, insert needle through first stitch on one side, draw under two strands along the edge, then work in same manner under two strands on opposite-side edge and continue in this manner, sewing from side to side until the seam is completely woven. A sewn seam is usually done with a blunt-edge tapestry needle and approximately a ¼-inch running backstitch on the wrong side of work. The crocheted seam is done with a fine crochet hook, on the wrong side of work, and with either a single crochet stitch or a slip stitch. A single crochet stitch is made by inserting the hook through both strands of the stitches along both side edges to be seamed, placing yarn over hook and drawing through the stitches, then yarn over again and drawing through the two loops on hook. A slip stitch is made by inserting the hook in both strands of both stitches, placing yarn over hook and drawing through the stitches and the one loop on hook.

Forming hemlines

Where a hem is desired, it is usually made with a turning ridge, which lends firmness to the shape of the hem. This generally occurs when the starting piece (which for a hem is often done on needles three sizes smaller than those used on the rest of the garment to avoid bulkiness) measures approximately 1 inch, and it is made by working a purl row on the right side of the work. A picot hemline is a variation of the more tailored one, and it is often used on infants' clothes and other types of garments that require a little bottom interest. It is made, after the starting piece measures approximately 1 inch, ending with a purl row, by working the next row as follows: Knit 1, * yarn over, knit 2 together, repeat from *. across row. The following row is again a purl row. When this type of hemline is worked, the bottom, after being sewn, has a firm scalloped edge.

Crochet edging on knitting

A crocheted edging is often used to finish off a piece of knitting, usually a single crocheted edging around the bottom, and very often a fancier one around other openings such as the neck or the front of a cardigan. The first row of any crocheted edging is a single crochet row worked color over color, with right side of work facing you, by inserting the hook through the top strand of the last or bound-off stitch to be worked, placing yarn over hook, drawing through the stitch, then yarn over again, and drawing through the two loops on hook. You do not work into every stitch but into only as many stitches as necessary to make sure that the work lies perfectly flat. Corners can be rounded out by shaping as you turn, or squared by working 3 single crochet stitches in each corner stitch as you turn.

Waistband casings

Waistband casings for the drawing through of elastic are generally done in one of two ways: the first a simple turn-under hem and the other a crocheted casing worked along the wrong side of a waistband. Of the two methods, the latter is the more desirable, since with it the garment is flatter at a place where it needs to be flatter. Crocheted casings are made as follows: Working on wrong side, attach yarn at one top end of waistband, work a slip stitch (see how to work a slip stitch under "Seaming" in this section), * chain the equivalent of 1 inch, slip stitch at bottom of waistband approximately ¾ inch beyond the last slip stitch, chain the equivalent of 1 inch, slip stitch at top of waistband approximately ¾ inch beyond last slip stitch, repeat from * across waistband and fasten off.

Shortening by drawing a thread

To shorten a knitted garment, select a point approximately ½ inch below the desired length, cut open a stitch at one end of work, right side facing, and draw out from across the entire row the thread of yarn cut at that point. All of the stitches on that last row after drawing the thread will remain, unconnected but solid and whole. Working with the same drawn thread now, rip out the next row slowly, stitch by stitch, inserting one of the two free knitting needles into each stitch as you rip. There is now a complete solid row of stitching on a needle at the desired length. At this point, bind off and work one or two rows of single-crochet around, or work a hemline and a hem, or a bottom edge of ribbing.

Ripping

Unfortunately, an error in knitting is sometimes discovered several rows after it has occurred. This calls for either a ripping job or choosing to overlook the error. To rip, which is to accept "first medicine" rather than to always be aware of the error, even though it may involve only one stitch, withdraw your needle, rip to one row below where the error occurred, then rip out the next row stitch by stitch, inserting one of the two free needles into each stitch as you go. You are now ready to continue with your knitting again.

Selvage edging

A selvage edge is often worked at either end of a flat piece of knitting where there will be no seaming and the piece is required to be firm at the sides when finished. It is also used along only one side of a garment when a vertical hemline is desired, such as for a facing at the front opening of a cardigan jacket. When it is to be worked on both sides, slip the first and last stitch of every other row, regardless of what the rest of the knitting pattern is; when it is to be worked for a vertical hemline on one side only, knit, starting on the right side of work, as many stitches as desired for the width of the hem, slip the next stitch, then complete the row in the usual manner, and repeat this every other row for the desired length of the vertical hemline.

Joining yarn

Joining a new ball of yarn should be done at the beginning or end of a row whenever possible, in spite of the fact that the old ball of yarn may run out in the middle or toward the end of the row and a small length of the yarn may be wasted. When this is not possible, for some reason, such as a shortage of yarn, work to within 3 or 4 inches of the end of the yarn, allow the same length end on the new ball, splice each end in half, twist them around each other to form one strand the equivalent thickness of the original yarn, then work the next 3 or 4 stitches with both strands, drop the old and continue with the new only. When the knitting is completed, weave about 1 inch of each of the remaining strands into the wrong side of work.

Duplicate stitch

Duplicate stitches are often embroidered in contrast color over stockinette stitch to form a design. Since the duplicate stitch is a copy of the stockinette stitch, it can also be used in same color as a mending stitch. It is done by inserting a blunt-edge tapestry needle from the wrong side through the center of the V stockinette stitch and working over the left and right diagonal lines of that stitch. Be careful not to pull the stitches too tightly in order to avoid a puckering in the work.

Front bands for cardigans

Usually the bottom of a cardigan sweater is worked in a stitch different from the body of the garment, more often than not a 2- or 3-inch ribbing worked on needles three sizes smaller than those used on the rest of the sweater in order to give it some shape and differentiate it from a jacket. When this is done, and you want to have the front bands in the same stitch as the bottom, work the ribbed portion for the desired length of the bottom border, then slip the number of stitches at one end necessary for the front band onto a pin to be worked later, and continue with the remaining stitches in the pattern and with the needles chosen for the body of the sweater. When this is completed, slip the stitches from the pin onto the smaller needles again and continue with the ribbing for the front band until the piece measures the same length as the rest of the garment. This separate piece is later seamed to the front of the sweater.

Blocking

Blocking, the final finish to your knitted garment, may be done before or after the pieces are assembled. With the work laid flat, cover it with a damp cloth and press lightly, allowing steam to form. Avoid pressing hard or holding the iron too long in any one place. When done, measure the piece to be sure it is the proper size. If it should need a little stretch in any direction at this time, do it while the garment is still damp, and then repeat the pressing process.

8

Designer's guide

In practically all crafts, there are certain rules that should be observed in order to make everything come out just right. So it is, too, for designing one's own knitwear. Basic rules for proportion and shaping should be followed or at least employed as guidelines for whatever variation you choose to use in the designing of your own garments. Outlined here alphabetically for easy reference are most of the things that will be of greatest value to you in your new venture into the field of knitting design. So that you may have examples, let us assume that what you are making is being worked on a gauge of 5 stitches and 7 rows to 1 inch, knowing by now (after reading our "How to Design" chapter) that if your stitch and row gauge are different, you will have to vary your calculations. Here also are standard body-size measurement charts, which serve as guidelines for whatever you are making. Keep in mind that if your own measurements vary somewhat from the suggested sizes given, you will need to adjust the calculations for your design, and also that allowances will have to be made for seaming (see Knitter's Guide) and for ease of fit for certain types of garments, such as jackets, coats, and other loose-fitting articles of clothing.

Standard body-size measurements

BABY AND TODDLER SIZES

Sizes	6 mos.	1	2	3	4
Chest	19"	20"	21"	22"	23"
Underarm length	6½"	7"	7½"	8"	9"
Armhole	4"	4¼"	4½"	4¾"	5"
Sleeve width	6½"	7½"	8"	8½"	9"
Sleeve length	6½"	7½"	8½"	9½"	10½"
Shoulder back	8¾"	9"	9¼"	9½"	9¾"
Crotch length	6½"	7"	7½"	8"	8½"
Waist	18"	19"	20"	21"	22"

CHILDREN'S SIZES

Sizes	4	6	8	10	12
Chest	23"	24"	26"	28"	30"
Shoulder back	9¾"	10¼"	10¾"	11¼"	12"
Shoulder	2¾"	3"	3¼"	3½"	3¾"
Back of neck	4¼"	4¼"	4¼"	4¼"	4½"
Armhole depth	4½"	5"	5½"	6"	6½"
Bottom to underarm	9"	10"	11"	11½"	12"
Underarm sleeve length	10½"	11½"	12½"	13½"	15"
Sleeve width at underarm	9"	9½"	10"	11"	11½"

JUNIOR SIZES

Sizes	9	11	13	15
Bust	31″	33″	35″	37″
Waist	22″	23″	24″	25″
Shoulder back	11½″	12¼″	13″	13¼″
Back of neck	4″	4¼″	4½″	4¾″
Shoulder	3¾″	4″	4¼″	4½″
Armhole depth	6¾″	7″	7¼″	7½″
Waist to underarm	7″	7½″	7½″	8″
Underarm sleeve length	17″	17″	17½″	17½″
Sleeve width at underarm	11½″	12″	12″	12½″

WOMEN'S SIZES

Sizes	10	12	14	16	18	20
Bust	32″	34″	36″	38″	40″	42″
Waist	24″	25″	26″	28″	30″	32″
Hip	33″	35″	37″	39″	41″	43″
Shoulder back	12¼″	13″	13¾″	14½″	15¼″	16″
Shoulder	4″	4¼″	4½″	4¾″	5″	5¼″
Back of neck	4¼″	4½″	4¾″	5″	5¼″	5½″
Armhole depth	7″	7¼″	7½″	7¾″	8″	8¼″
Waist to underarm	7½″	8″	8″	8½″	8½″	8½″
Underarm sleeve length	17½″	18″	18″	18½″	18½″	18½″
Sleeve width at underarm	11½″	12″	12½″	13″	13½″	14″

Sizes	Slipover			Sleeveless		
	Small (26–28)	Medium (30–32)	Large (34–36)	Small (26–28)	Medium (30–32)	Large (34–36)
Chest	27″	31″	35″	27″	31″	35″
Shoulder back	11″	12″	13″	10″	11″	12″
Back of neck	4½″	4½″	5″	4½″	4½″	5″
Shoulder	3¼″	3¾″	4″	2¾″	3¼″	3½″
Armhole depth	6½″	7″	7½″	7½″	8″	8½″
Length to underarm	11″	12½″	14″	10½″	11″	12½″
Sleeve width	11″	11½″	12″			
Sleeve length	14″	15½″	17″			

Sizes	Slipover			Sleeveless		
	Small (36–38)	Medium (40–42)	Large (44–46)	Small (36–38)	Medium (40–42)	Large (44–46)
Chest	37″	41″	45″	37″	41″	45″
Shoulder back	16″	17″	18″	15″	16″	17″
Shoulder	5″	5½″	6″	4¼″	5″	5½″
Back of neck	6″	6″	6″	6″	6″	6″
Armhole depth	8½″	9″	9½″	9½″	10″	10½″
Length to underarm	15″	15½″	15½″	13″	13½″	13½″
Sleeve width	15″	16″	17″			
Sleeve length	19″	19¼″	19½″			

A-line shaping

Regardless of the degree of A-line shaping you want to use in your coat, blouse, dress, or skirt, the basic rule is that the shaping should be gradual rather than jagged. Depending on the styling you are working, A-lines generally vary from between 1 and 3 inches in width on each side for a short garment and up to 6 inches on longer ones. If your total decreasing is to be done in an area of 6 inches (42 rows), and you are having a 2-inch A-line shape on each side, you would need to reduce 10 stitches at each end of needle on both the back and front of your garment. Working at the 5 stitch and 7 row to 1 inch gauge, you would decrease 1 stitch at the beginning and end of every 4th row 9 times, then every 6th row once; and if you are planning a 1-inch A-line in an area of 4 inches

(28 rows), you would decrease 1 stitch at the beginning and end of every 4th row once, then every 6th row 4 times.

Afghans

Most afghans are rectangular in shape, and usually a minimum of 12 inches and a maximum of 20 inches longer than they are wide. A minimum width of 48 inches and a maximum of 72 inches, and a minimum length of 58 inches and a maximum of 90 inches generally fall into the category of most desirable sizes. Since even the smallest of afghans is a large piece, they are practically always worked in sections, either strips or squares, and then the sections are joined together to form the total piece by either weaving or sewing a thin seam, or with the use of a row of single crochet or slip stitch along either the right or wrong side of work. Crochet joining on the wrong side makes an inconspicuous seam, and on the right side an exaggerated seam. Often the latter method, when worked in a contrast color, adds much interest to the general pattern of the afghan itself. In any case, when a crocheted joining is used, there should be a row of single crochet first around each piece, so that the final joinings are even and lie perfectly flat and smooth, and this first row should be in color over color for a neater finish.

When an afghan is finally joined and completed, there is usually a border and trim around the entire outer edge. This final finish might be a single crochet border in contrast or self color, or a fringed border, plain or fancy, or a chain-loop crocheted straight or ruffled edging. Whichever finish is used, always there is first a row or two of single crochet, color over color, around the entire edge of the finished piece, squaring out the corners and making the shape of the afghan firm and solid. For further information on how to design, calculate, and final finish afghans, see How to Design (Chapter 5), and for information on crocheted edges in knitting, see the Knitter's Guide (Chapter 7).

Armhole shaping

The shaping of armholes generally falls into two categories, that for the set-in sleeve and that for the raglan. As in all other shaping, the process must be a gradual one. For regulation armholes, shaping begins at the start of armhole depth and is generally worked by starting on the right side of work and binding off the number of stitches equivalent to between 1 and 1½ inches at the beginning of each of the next 2 rows, then decreasing 1 stitch at the beginning and end of every other row until the shaping is completed. To determine the number of stitches involved in the complete shaping of both armholes on the back of your garment, you would calculate as follows: Subtract from the total number of stitches the number you will need remaining for the two shoulders and the back of the neck. This will tell you how many stitches you will use in the complete armhole shaping. Let us assume that the back of your garment measures 16 inches, each of the shoulders measures 4 inches, and the back of the neck measures 4¼ inches. Calculated to our presumed gauge, you are working on approximately 80 stitches (this figure possibly varying slightly, depending on the multiple of your pattern stitch) at the point where the armhole shaping begins. When you are done with the armhole shaping, you should have remaining the necessary number of stitches to complete both shoulders and the back of neck. In this case it would be 20 + 22 + 20 = 62. Subtract 62 from 80, and you are left with the number of stitches to be bound off for your armholes. 80 minus 62 = 18. Half of 18 for each armhole = 9. You would probably shape your back armholes as follows: Bind off 6 stitches at beginning of each of the next 2 rows, then decrease 1 stitch at beginning and end of every other row 3 times. Front armholes are always shaped exactly like those on back.

Raglan armholes generally measure approximately 1 inch longer than the regulation ones and are decreased gradually, with either a small or no initial bind-off, until no stitches remain. There is no shoulder involved in a raglan, so you need to subtract only the back of neck measurement from the body measurement to determine the shaping of the raglan. With this type of armhole, you need to count your row gauge as well as your stitch gauge. If you are designing a garment the same size as the one worked out above, and the standard armhole measurement on that one is 7 inches, in this case the armhole would measure 8 inches. 80 stitches minus 22 (for back of neck) = 58 stitches. Divide this figure in half (for each armhole), and you have 29 stitches for the shaping on each side. Since the armhole is to measure 8 inches, you would multiply 8 by 7 (number of rows per inch) and find that you have 56 rows, with, let us say, a 3-stitch initial bind-off. Raglan shaping at this point is a little more complicated than other sleeve shapings, since you need to know how you can most gradually decrease the necessary number of stitches in the given number of rows, and there is no leeway allowed for not having decreased all your stitches by the time you have reached your full armhole depth. In this case, you would look for the nearest multiple of 29 less 3, for initial bind-off, in 56 less 2 for the 8-inch armhole. $26 \times 2 = 52$, which is about as close as you can get with the multiple. You would probably shape your raglan armholes as follows: Bind off 3 stitches at beginning and end of the next 2 rows, then 1 stitch at beginning and end of every 4th row once, then every other row 25 times. By doing this you will have decreased the 26 stitches in 54 rows, and you

will have designed a good-fitting, well-shaped raglan armhole.

Buttonhole placements

Our Knitter's Guide chapter describes how to form buttonholes, but in designing, you should be aware of the generally accepted rules for their placement. On cardigan sweaters the first buttonhole is usually formed when the piece measures 1 inch (most garments are worked from the bottom up), the last one 1 inch below the start of the neckline (regardless of its shape), and the remaining ones spaced evenly between. On jackets and short coats, the first one usually occurs when your work measures between 8 and 10 inches. On longer garments, the placement of the first buttonhole is generally between 12 and 18 inches from the bottom. In all instances, the top one occurs 1 inch below the start of neck shaping, except perhaps where very large buttons are being used, and in that case you would probably start that last buttonhole ½ to 1 inch lower to accommodate the extra circumference on the button. Usually buttonholes are placed about 1 inch in from the front edge, and on double-breasted garments a space of between 3½ and 5 inches is generally allowed between the two sets of buttonholes.

Capes and ponchos

These types of garments are usually knitted from the top down. Shaping is still gradual, although it needs to be calculated carefully, since the top neck and shoulder portion is much smaller than the full bottom width, and increases need to occur at the proper places so that the piece grows as necessary to achieve correct measurements from neck to bust, to bottom fullness. To clarify, a good-fitting garment of this type with a 12-inch circumference for neck opening, a 36-inch circumference at the bust, and an 88-inch circumference at the bottom might allow 7 inches in which you must grade from the top to the bust measurement, and 23 inches from that point to the bottom—the total length from top to bottom being, let us say, 30 inches. In a presumed gauge of 5 stitches and 7 rows to 1 inch, we would start out with 60 stitches at the neck, graduating to 180 stitches in the first 50 rows to the bust, and then to 440 stitches for full width in 160 rows. That is as many rows as you need to the point when you want your full width to occur, which is often approximately 5 to 6 inches above the bottom, or in this case, 40 rows less than the full 160 rows. 180 minus 60 = 120, which is the number of stitches you will need to increase in your first 50 rows, and 440 minus 180 = 260, which is the number of stitches you will need to increase in your next 120 rows.

You would probably work your garment in this manner: Cast on 60 stitches. Work even for ½ inch, then increase 10 stitches evenly spaced every 4th row 12 times, making a total of 120 stitches increased in 48 rows. You now have 180 stitches increased in approximately 50 rows, and a bust measurement of 36 inches; your piece is 7 inches long. You now need to increase 260 stitches in the next 120 rows to achieve full width and proper length. It would be best now to continue to increase 10 stitches every 4th row 18 times more, and then 10 stitches every 6th row 8 times. You now have increased the additional 260 stitches in 120 rows, and you have reached full width to a point 5 inches above the total length of your garment, and would work even for those remaining 5 inches. **Note:** In working these types of garments, the top is usually done in one piece. Then the work is divided into either two or four sections soon after the full bust measurement has been reached, and

then seamed in the final finish. This is done because the total number of stitches becomes quite large as you work down, and it is unwieldy to work in one piece.

Cardigans

Cardigans are usually made by working the garment in five parts, and then adding the finish. The back is worked first, then each of the two fronts, and finally the sleeves. Each front is worked to measure half the size of the back, plus whatever stitches need to be added for overlap. For instance, if you have the usual single set of buttonholes, which are generally placed 1 inch in from center front, you would need to add that inch to each of your cardigan fronts. If, on the other hand, you are designing your cardigan with a double-breasted set of double buttonholes, having, for example, a 5-inch overlap, you would need to divide that 5 inches in half and add 2½ inches to each front. Another rule for the designing of cardigans is that, as an open sweater and very often a casual type of garment meant to be worn over something like a blouse or a slipover, it should be made 1 inch wider all around, and the armholes should be made ½ to 1 inch deeper than regulation. This will provide the ease of fit necessary for this type of garment.

Coats and jackets

Rules for cardigans generally apply to coats and jackets as well, with the exception that these garments are always designed to be worn over other clothing and must allow for that fact. Also, they are never as tight-fitting as a sweater of any type. Using basic measurements to start with, between 2 and 5 inches should be allowed for extra width of both body and sleeves, and an extra 1½ to 3 inches for armhole depth. The placement of buttons and buttonholes also varies a little from that on cardigans. For a knowledge of this, refer to the general information on buttonholes earlier in this chapter.

Gathering

When gathering is included in a design, whether it be for a full dirndl skirt, a peplum, a hat brim, or any other project involving a degree of fullness or ruffle at some point, designer's rules state that average gathering requires double the starting width, moderate gathering one-half the starting width, and very full gathering three times the starting width. Any of these proportions can be easily achieved in knitting, and the method is to increase the necessary number of stitches at the point where gathering is to occur. Unlike any other shaping, gathering requires almost an immediate form, rather than the more gradual one that occurs in most other types of shaping. If an average gathering is desired, the number of stitches on the needle would be doubled. For a moderate gathering, one-half again the number of starting stitches would be added, and for a very full gathering the number would be tripled. Since most shaping turns out best when it is started on the right side of the work, and most increasing and decreasing is best done on an all-knit row, regardless of the pattern stitch involved in the rest of the design, average gathering would be made by knitting and increasing 1 stitch in each stitch across the first row, and then working even. For how to increase, refer to our Knitter's Guide. For a moderate gathering, increase 1 stitch in every other stitch across the row in the same manner. A triple increase involves a little variation, because by increasing 2 stitches in each stitch across, you would be apt to pull or stretch your original first stitch out of shape, and thus form gaps, or small holes, in your work. In this case, then, where a triple increase is involved, it is best to work it in a double procedure, increasing 1 stitch in every stitch across the first row, and then 1 in every other stitch on the next row. Should the gathering occur first, followed by your straight work, you would decrease at the end of the ruffle in the same manner as you would have increased if it had occurred at the end.

Hat shaping

Knitted hats can be worked either from the top down or the bottom up. Although they are round, they are more often than not worked on a pair of straight needles, rather than on a round needle or a set of double-pointed needles, and then seamed at the back. This makes for easier handling and less difficulty in the shaping process. The top starting point of a hat measures about 1 or 1½ inches, and the bottom 3 inches less than the circumference of your head at a point approximately 1 inch below the top of your ears. The reason for using 3 inches less than the actual measurement is that there is a lot of stretch to knitted hats, and to fit properly they should be snug to the head. Hats can be made in any type of stitch, ranging from the basic stockinette to a simple rib, an interesting texture, or a cable twist. Regardless of the pattern involved, however, your increases or decreases, depending on whether you are working from the top down or the bottom up, work out best when done on a knit row. The bottom of a hat is generally finished after the rest of the hat is completed, and if there is no brim or peak or other bottom trim, there should be a small hem (on the wrong side of work), a ribbed edging, or a row or two of single crochet, worked loosely so that it does not bind the hat at the bottom. Shaping at the top of the crown can be worked either gradually over a space of 3 or 4 inches, or more rapidly over a space of 1 or 2 inches, this depending on the style of hat you are making.

As an example of how to start knitting a hat, let us assume that you want to make a basic pull-on type, in a small all-over textured stitch with a multiple of 4, and in our testing gauge of 5 stitches and 7 rows to an inch. First you would measure your head at the widest point just below the top of your ears. If your measurement is 21 inches, which is average adult size, you would plan your hat to measure 18 inches at that point. 18 multiplied by your gauge of 5 stitches to 1 inch would be 90, to which you need to add 2 more stitches to accommodate to your pattern multiple. If you decide to work from the bottom up, you would cast on 92 stitches and work even in your pattern for the length you want, depending on the depth of the hat you are making, and the style, which will tell you if the top shaping should be done gradually in, let us say 4 inches, or more rapidly in 2 inches. If you want a gradual shaping, you would probably work on your 92 stitches until your piece measures 4 inches (or 28 rows) less than the desired depth, ending with a wrong-side row; then you would change to stockinette stitch and decrease 6 stitches evenly spaced on every other row 14 times, thus reducing your width to approximately 1½ inches in 8 rows. At this point you would break off your yarn, leaving a long thread, and draw the thread tightly through the remaining stitches left on needle. On the other hand, if you wanted a rapid shaping to be worked in about 2 inches, you would change to stockinette stitch when your piece measures 2 inches (or 14 rows) less than the desired depth, and would probably decrease 12 stitches evenly spaced every other row 7 times, and then fasten off as before. In this same manner of shaping, if you were working your hat from the top down, you would reverse the process and cast on 8 stitches, then increase in the same manner as you decreased until you reach 92 stitches, from which point on you would work

even. If a brim or other bottom trim is to be added, you would do it now, before sewing the back seam and blocking your hat into shape. By the same token, if a bottom edge is to be put on, you would also do this just before final finishing.

A few more guides on variations in hats follow here. Berets and tams, at their widest point, are usually double the width of the 3 inches less than your actual head measurement, though they start or end, depending again on whether you are working from bottom up or top down, with the regulation 3 inches less than actual head measurement, this for your band, which usually measures between 1½ and 2 inches deep. The increase or decrease in number of stitches between the band and the widest portion of the beret occurs rapidly, as in the other types of gathering described in an earlier paragraph in this chapter, and the increasing or decreasing, depending on which method is being used, begins about 1 inch above the bottom of the beret fullness.

Stocking caps are worked in the same manner as other hats, except that decreasing or increasing, as the case may be, is worked very gradually in order to span the difference in the number of stitches between the widest part and the two- or three-stitch point which drops to the back of the cap in a space of usually between 12 and 15 inches. For example, in our presumed gauge, the widest portion of your cap would be worked on 90 stitches. In order to drop to the very few stitches you need in the span of 12 inches, or approximately 84 rows, you would probably decrease 1 stitch at the beginning and end of every other row 42 times and, remaining with 6 stitches, you would work off 2 stitches as 1 across the next row and then bind off. Again, if your drop would be 15 inches, or approximately 106 rows, you would decrease 1 stitch at each end of needle every 4th row 10 times, then every other row 32 times.

Straight brims are worked in the same direction as the rest of the hat, whether from the top down or the bottom up. The bottom of the brim is usually between 1½ and 2 inches wider than the top of it, and the shaping for this occurs within the first 3 or 4 rows beyond the point where the top of the brim meets the bottom of the crown. Extra firm brims are often worked either with double yarn for body or with a full turn-under hem, shaped in reverse to the top of the brim. A soft ruffled brim is worked, again, either from top down or bottom up, and the ruffling is achieved in the same manner as all other gathering, described earlier.

In turn-over cuffs, except if worked in one of the few stitches that are exactly the same on both sides, such as straight ribbing or garter stitch, the portion of the bottom of the hat to be cuffed over needs to be worked in reverse to the rest of the hat. In working down, a good method is to bind off loosely at the bottom, then pick up your stitches on the *wrong* side of work, and work again in your pattern for the desired depth of cuff. In working from the bottom up, you would probably start out with your pattern stitch, work to the desired depth of cuff, ending with a right-side row, then reverse your pattern on the next row. In this way, the cuff, when turned over, will match the top portion of your hat.

Peaks on hats are made like brims, except that they are worked on only the front half of the hat. They are always added after the balance of the hat has been completed and are shaped to a gradual, narrow roundness at the bottom.

Neck shaping

There are many styles of neck shaping, the most popular being the round neck, the V-neck, the scoop neck, and the boat neck. Round necks, including those with turtleneck collars, and V-necks have the regulation neck and shoulder shaping on the back. A round neck shaping on the front of a sweater occurs 2 inches below the start of shoulder shaping, and the number of stitches to be calculated in the shaping of the round neck is the number of stitches remaining on the needle, less those required for both shoulders. The shaping is usually done by working both sides of the neck at once, with a center bind-off, and then three gradual decreases on either side of the neck opening. For example, if you have after armhole shaping 64 stitches on your needle (ending, as for most shaping, on the wrong side of work), your piece measures 2 inches less than the depth of the armhole, and you need a total of 40 stitches remaining for both shoulders, you would shape your neck as follows: Work across 23 stitches, join another ball of yarn, bind off the next 18 stitches, then complete your row as you started on the remaining 23 stitches. Working now on both sides at once, decrease 1 stitch at each neck edge every other row 3 times, then work even on 20 stitches of each side until the piece measures same as back to shoulders, then shape shoulders as on back.

On a V-neck there is the same number of stitches to work with, but the start of the neck shaping occurs much lower and, still working on both sides at once, the shaping would be quite different. V-neck shapings can begin at any point, but the average one, on a right-side row again, starts just after the completion of the armhole shaping. For example, as on the round neck, there are 64 stitches on your needle, and you need to have 40 for your shoulders; since in V-neck shapings you count rows, and you have approximately 6 inches, or 42 rows, to work with, you would proceed as follows: Knit across 32 stitches, join another ball of yarn, and knit across remaining 32 stitches. Working on both sides at once, at each neck edge decrease 1 stitch every 4th row 9 times, and every other row 3 times. When piece measures same as back to shoulders, shape your shoulders as on back.

Scoop necks are often the same for both front and back, although sometimes the styling might involve the regulation high neck at back and a scoop in the front only. The depth of this type of shaping is a complete variable, entirely up to your own discretion, although the average scoop occurs approximately 2 inches above the end of the armhole shaping and generally, by virtue of its width, narrows each of the shoulders by about 1½ inches. Assuming that each of the shoulders in this case requires 14 stitches, and you have on your needle 64 stitches after the armhole shaping has been completed, you would subtract 28 (two shoulders) from 64 and be left with 36, which is the number of stitches to be worked in your neck shaping. You would probably work as follows: Knit across 19 stitches, join another ball of yarn, bind off the center 26 stitches, then work across the remaining 19 stitches. Working on both sides at once, decrease 1 stitch at each neck edge every other row 5 times, then knit 14 stitches of each side until piece measures same as back to shoulders, if the back is regulation length, or whatever armhole measurement is required for the size garment you are making if the back is shaped the same as the front. The shoulder bind-off is the same as the back shoulder bind-off.

Boat necks are quite simple to make, and there is never a variation between the shaping of the front and back of the garment. A boat neck is high and wide, and narrows the shoulders by the extra 3 or 4 inches absorbed by its width. In designing the boat neck, work to 2 rows before the start of the shoulder shaping, work across the foreshortened shoulder stitches, join another ball of yarn, bind off the elongated neck stitches, then work across the other shoulder stitches. Working on both sides at once, work 1 row even and then bind off for the shoulders as necessary. Probably in the final finishing of this garment, you would work a row or two of single crochet around the neck opening after the shoulder seams have been sewn. If you want a narrow ribbed finish around the neck, you would start the shaping about 1 inch below the start of the shoulders, slip the center neck stitches onto a spare needle, and, after the shoulder shaping has been completed, work in ribbing for 1 inch across the stitches on the spare needle.

Shoulder shaping

The shaping of shoulders is a relatively simple procedure, started always on the right side of the work after the armhole depth has been reached. The one point to remember is that shoulders should be worked gradually in order to have the proper shape, generally in two steps where a maximum of 24 stitches is involved for each shoulder, and in three steps where there are more. For example, if there are 24 stitches to be bound off for each shoulder on the back of a garment, you would probably work as follows: When piece measures desired length to shoulders, ending with a wrong-side row, bind off 12 stitches at the beginning of each of the next 4 rows, and then bind off (always loosely) the remaining stitches for the back of neck. If there are 34 stitches, bind off 11 at the beginning of each of the next 4 rows, 12 at the beginning of the next 2 rows, and then bind off the remaining stitches for the back of neck.

Sleeve shapings

A regulation long set-in sleeve, usually worked up from the bottom, starts with the wrist measurement and a ribbed cuff of between 2 and 3 inches, generally worked in needles three times smaller than those used on the rest of the sleeve. The pattern stitch starts at the completion of the cuff, at which time you change to the needles you have been using for the rest of the garment, and begin to increase at each side of work at gradual intervals to the width required for the underarm sleeve measurement. From that point on, you work even until the sleeve measures desired length to underarm, and then you shape the cap. To shape a cap, at beginning of each of the next 2 rows, bind off the same number of stitches as at armhole bind-off on front and back of the garment, then decrease 1 stitch at the beginning and end of every other row until the cap measures 3 inches less than the total armhole depth. You then bind off the necessary number of stitches at the beginning of each of the next 4 or 6 rows so that the number of stitches remaining measures between 1 inch and 1½ inches, and possibly 2 inches. These stitches become your final bind-off. This method of shaping the cap of a set-in sleeve always remains the same, regardless of the length or style of the rest of the sleeve.

Raglan sleeves are worked in the same manner as set-in sleeves to the point where the cap shaping begins. In shaping the raglan cap, the initial bind-off is again the same as that on the back and front of the garment; then you begin to decrease 1 stitch at the beginning and end of every other row, con-forming as closely as possible to the shape and length of the raglan shaping on the armholes. When piece measures about 2 to 2½ inches less than the full length of the armhole, count the number of stitches remaining, then decrease either more or less rapidly, depending on the number of stitches involved, so that the cap will measure, when completed, the same as the armhole, and there are remaining the equivalent number of stitches to approximate 1 inch. These stitches become your final bind-off.

Slipovers

Most all pullover sweaters are worked with exactly the same number of stitches on both back and front, which is that number necessary for the bust or chest measurement, divided in half. Except in instances where there is a different pattern stitch styling on the front, both pieces are worked exactly the same to the point where neck shaping begins.

Translation of knitting terms

American		Spanish	French	German	Italian
Decrease	(dec)	disminuir	diminution	abnehmen	diminuire
Double point	(dp)	punto doble	d'aiguilles	hilssnadeln	doppio punto
Increase	(inc)	aumentar	augmentation	aufnehmen	aumentare
Knit	(k)	derecho	endroit	rechte	diritto
Pass slip stitch over	(psso)	pasar punto sobre otro	surjet	abgehobene über die gestrickte	accavallamento
Pattern	(pat)	patron	point	muster	punto
Purl	(p)	reves	envers	linke	rovescio
Repeat	(rep)	repetir	reprendre	wiederholen	riprendere
Slip	(sl)	pasar sin trabajando	glisser	abheben	passare
Stitch	(st)	malla	maille	masche	maglia
Together	(tog)	junto	ensemble	zusammen	insieme
Yarn over	(yo)	hilo sobre la aguja	jeté	umschlag	gettato

Index